AF394364

To Break and To Branch

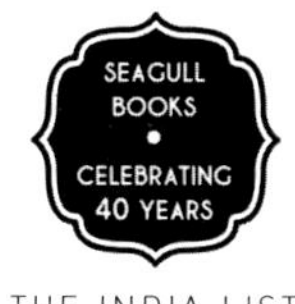

THE INDIA LIST

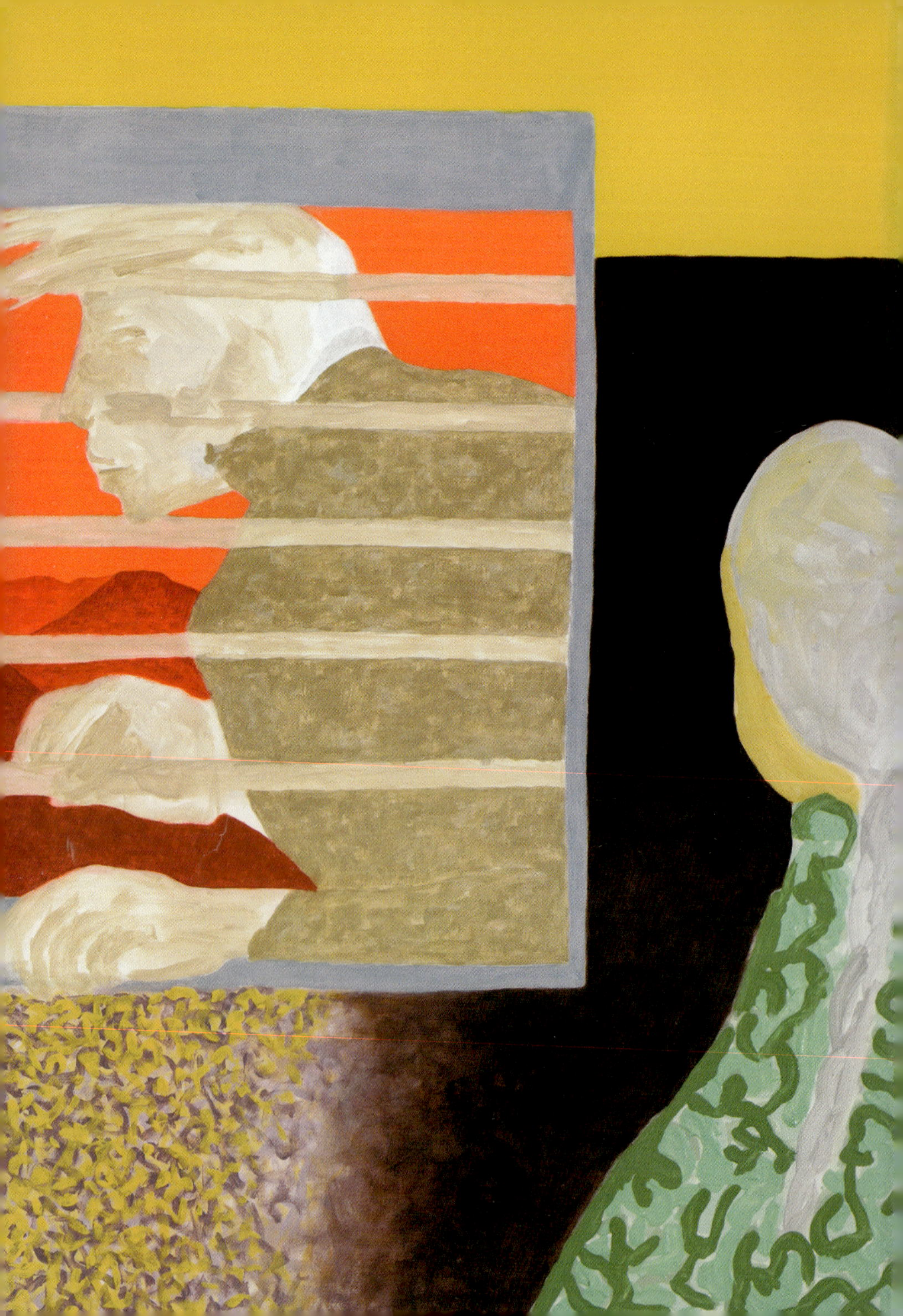

To Break and To Branch

SIX ESSAYS ON GIEVE PATEL

Ranjit Hoskote

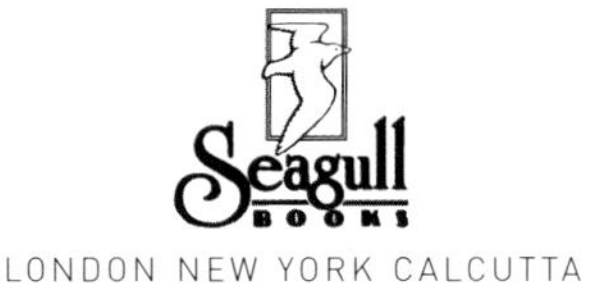

LONDON NEW YORK CALCUTTA

Seagull Books, 2024

This compilation © Seagull Books, 2024

Texts © Ranjit Hoskote

Gieve Patel's work © Avaan Patel

ISBN   978 1 80309 432 8

British Library Cataloguing-in-Publication Data

A catalogue record for this book is available from the British Library

Typeset and designed by Sunandini Banerjee, Seagull Books, Calcutta, India

Printed and bound in India by Hyam Enterprises, Calcutta, India

CONTENTS

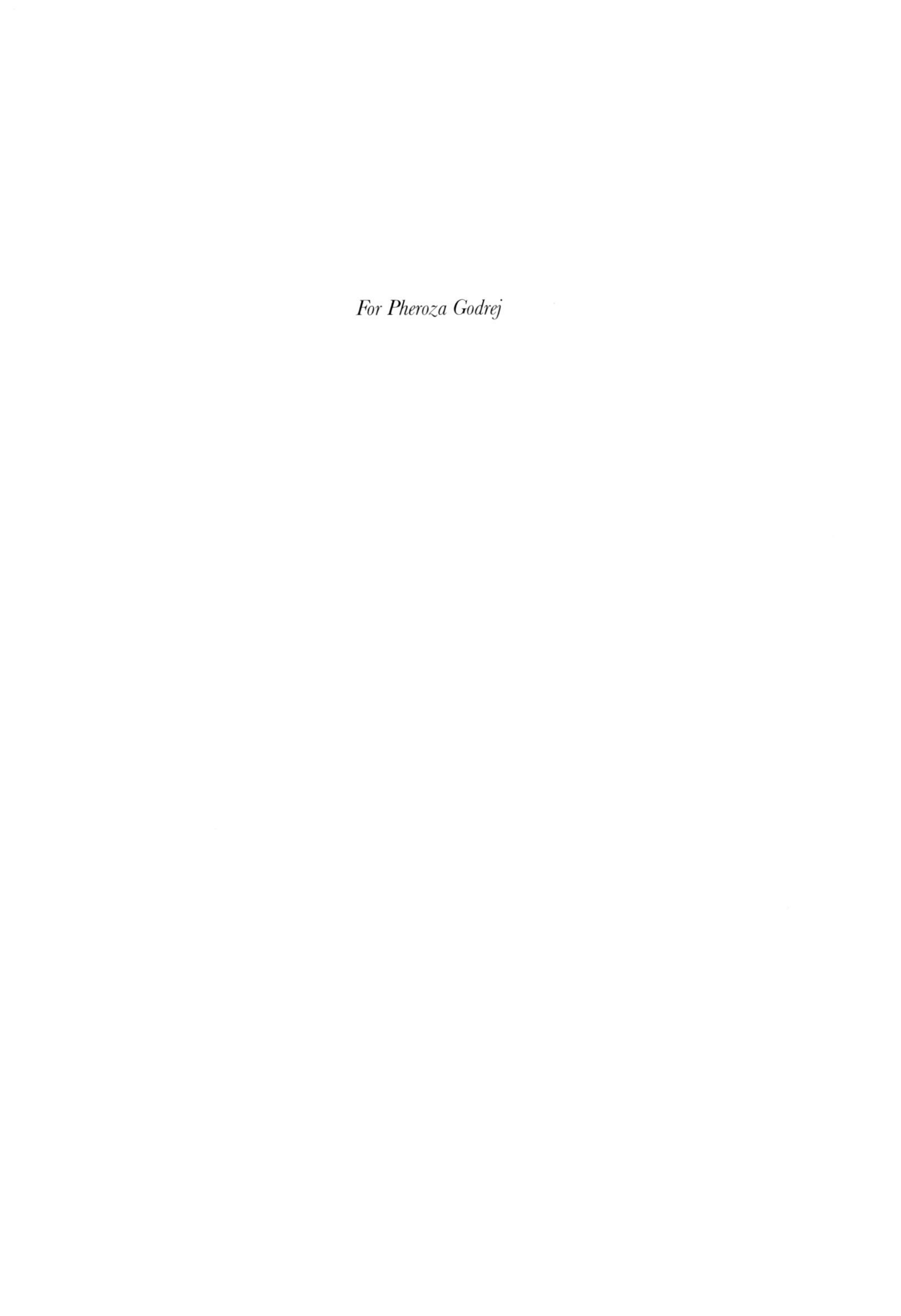

For Pheroza Godrej

Gieve and I: An Introduction

How does one summarize, or bear adequate witness to, a friendship that spanned 37 years? I was 18 when I first met Gieve Patel, at our guru Nissim Ezekiel's fabled office on the ground floor of Theosophy Hall in South Bombay. We represented two different generations of Nissim's acolytes. The Rabbi, as I used to call him, only half in jest—the teacher was blended, in his personality, with the sceptic questing for wisdom, the healer seeking to mend the world's brokenness and his own—had published Gieve's first book of poems in 1966 (titled, simply, *Poems*) under his own imprint. A quarter of a century later, in 1991, he would publish my first book of poems (rather more dramatically titled *Zones of Assault*) in Rupa & Co's New Poetry Series, which he edited.

I had already read Gieve's celebrated poem 'On Killing a Tree', of course: it featured in one of our high-school poetry textbooks, *Panorama*, published by the Oxford University Press. The poem's sharp-edged tonality, its stoic irony and momentous sense of the tragic within the everyday—these qualities survived our teachers' valiant efforts to domesticate it into a sententious cautionary tale. Gieve and I exchanged numbers and addresses, and soon began to correspond and speak over the phone.

How swiftly the forms of communication that we then used have been consigned to the Museum of Superseded Technologies: the inland letter and the rotary-dial landline. Yet the thoughts expressed and the ideas discussed, the mutual trust that sprang up intuitively, the warmth of that friendship—all these remain as inspiring and invigorating now as they were then.

Over the nearly four decades since we first met, Gieve and I would present our poems together at readings, serve collegially on juries and committees, chair each other's lectures or readings, hold public discussions on art and speak on art criticism panels together (he had been my predecessor as art critic to the *Times of India*, by many years). Nancy Adajania and I would make relatively more professional studio visits as well as regular, civilian visits to him, either at Malabar Apartments or, in later years, Cusrow Baug. Sometimes, I would drop by at his Lamington Road clinic, immortalized in a painting by his fellow Bombay artist Atul Dodiya. From Malabar Apartments, we would go on long walks in the Hanging Gardens, speaking of poetry, philosophy, art, and sharing plain old-fashioned gossip. At Cusrow Baug, we would circle this elegantly laid- out precinct designed by Claude Batley, the English architect who came to Bombay as a young man and made it his home. We would pause to remark on a tree here, a bird there—and the Baug's fire temple, its architecture and statuary intriguingly melded from art deco and futurism, faintly reminiscent of the edifices that dominate Fritz Lang's 1927 cinematic masterpiece, *Metropolis*. We travelled together to Jaipur when Gieve was working on his sculptures there, went to several editions of the lively Goa Arts and Literature Festival together and to Venice with a group of common friends.

When Nancy and I co-curated *No Parsi is an Island* at the National Gallery of Modern Art (NGMA), Bombay—as part of a constellation of exhibitions proposed by visionary scholar-patron Pheroza Godrej—Gieve was one of the 14 artists whose work we included; his expanded practice was one of the anchors of our show. We presented him in his creative fullness, with a series of his paintings from the series, *On Looking into a Well*, drawings of clouds, sculptures based on the twin themes of Eklavya and Daphne, archival black-and-white photographs from various performances of his plays, and—as a banner-like manifesto on the wall of the NGMA's rotunda—his urgent, politically searing poem, 'The Ambiguous Fate of Gieve Patel, He Being Neither Muslim nor Hindu in India'. Alongside his work, we displayed works by his (and our) dear friends Sudhir Patwardhan, Atul Dodiya and Anju Dodiya. Truly, this Parsi was no island.

I was privileged to be Gieve's friend, his fellow poet and a pilgrim accompanying him on his journey as a painter. Over a nearly 20-year period, from 2000 to 2018, I contributed essays to the catalogues that accompanied the periodic exhibitions of his work; these six essays have been brought together to form the present book.

*

Gieve's engagement with the arts was wide as well as deep, ranging across poetry and fiction, theatre and cinema, painting and sculpture, Western as well as Hindustani classical music, and dance. In every art, he found himself attracted to the virtuoso's flawless command over technique—yet he was also greatly moved by the more experimental practitioner's con brio gift for discovery and openness to revelation. Nothing was ever entirely fortuitous in Gieve's understanding of the world of imaginative endeavour: he prized the role that training played in an artist's refinement of intuition, the preparation that brought an artist to the threshold of unasked epiphany. Correspondingly, art works spoke best to him when they could be parsed through the intricate, replenishing interplay between expression and context.

Gieve's mentor in the visual arts was Akbar Padamsee, a major polymathic artist from the first generation of postcolonial Indian artists; Akbar was immersed in the study of Sanskrit and mathematics, and read French philosophers in the original. The paintings that Gieve showed in his first exhibition, held at the Jehangir Art Gallery, Bombay, in 1966, bore the impress of Akbar's style; this would soon change, although the two remained friends all their lives. In 1969, Akbar received the Jawaharlal Nehru Fellowship and used it to establish the Vision Exchange Workshop, a collaborative and transdisciplinary space that aimed to bring painting, cinema, psychoanalysis and literature into dialogue. He invited Gieve to join the Workshop; Gieve collaborated with the highly regarded cinematographer K. K. Mahajan to make a short film, *Chairs*, set in one of Bombay's Irani restaurants.

In 1975, the critic D. G. Nadkarni put Gieve in contact with Sudhir Patwardhan, suggesting that they might have much in common, as medical practitioners who were also artists—this marked the beginning of a close and enduring friendship. Gieve would introduce Sudhir to the circle of artists whose work he admired and whom he regarded as kindred spirits, including, among others, Bhupen Khakhar, Gulammohammed Sheikh and Vivan Sundaram. This circle, which also included the already influential art critic Geeta Kapur, is often loosely described as the 'Baroda group'; in fact, it had its moorings in Baroda, Bombay and Delhi, and announced the advent of a new, pan-Indian generation of artists. They had renounced the transcendental tonality and abstractionist preferences of the previous generation, in favour of a thoroughgoing engagement with the local and immediate. Each of these artists, in their distinctive manner—some were more ideologically geared, others more playful—wished to represent the protagonists and scenarios of everyday, unromanticized middle- and working-class life, until then largely absent from the ambit of mainstream Indian modernism. In 1981, although Gieve had by then chosen to pursue these concerns independently of the circle, Sudhir was one of the artists included in the landmark, manifesto-like exhibition with which it mounted its challenge to the status quo, *Place for People*.

*

Much loved and admired as a painter and a poet, Gieve also made a seminal contribution to theatre. He wrote only three plays—*Princes* (1971), *Savaksa* (1982) and *Mr Behram* (1987)—and yet each one was compelling, even unsettling in its subtle psychological portraiture; each one was intense in its delineation of the human appetites, the ebb and flow of affection, power, desire and self-knowledge in human relation-ships. Theatre had long been a crucial venue for Gieve's creativity; his association with the stage began early, during his years as a medical student, when he signed up with the magisterial Ebrahim Alkazi's Theatre Unit. Alkazi's daughter Amal once told me how, one afternoon at their home at Vithal Court in 1961, the family found themselves dis-turbed by a rhythmic stomping on the terrace above. The terrace housed Alkazi's legendary Meghdoot open-air theatre, but the performances were scheduled for the evenings. Going upstairs cautiously to investigate, they found Gieve marching up and down, rehearsing for his role as the Messenger in *Medea*. To be precise, Alkazi himself was playing the Messenger; Gieve was his understudy and took his responsibility to the production seriously.

Gieve would go on to marry Toni—Antoinette Diniz, though no one ever used her given name or birth surname—who founded Stage Two, producing and directing plays for a number of years and holding theatre workshops. Her production of Gieve's *Mr Behram* was memorable, as was her production of Cyrus Mistry's *Doongaji House;* coincidentally, both plays were studies in waning power, decadence and social change set in the ethos of Gieve's birth community, the Parsis of Western India. This train of thought takes me back to my own days at Elphinstone College and the University of Bombay: as a student, I acted in two of Toni's enacted play readings, which were staged in Bombay and Poona. Many years later, their daughter Avaan would direct a triad of my own plays, showing them in Bombay, Delhi and elsewhere.

*

Gieve was the kind of friend you could turn to for advice, professional or personal, in the certain knowledge that his response would be carefully thought-out, measured and sensitive; he was never casual in addressing the problems and dilemmas that his friends brought to his door. I will never forget the advice he gave me when, as a young poet, I went to him with my anxieties about the directions opening before me: 'To write truly meaningful poetry, you have to go deep down, to where things are broken.' My allegiance, at that point, was to a baroque form of articulation, and—regrettably—this advice did not immediately resonate for me. In my defence, I was only in my mid-twenties; the arc of life has long since demonstrated to me, with incontrovertible force, the accuracy of his sage counsel.

Gieve's artist friends also profited from his meticulous reading of their work. I find myself thinking back to the brief and resonant text that he wrote for the brochure—as these publications were then known;

galleries did not routinely bring out the lavish catalogues that they now do—accompanying Atul Dodiya's debut solo exhibition at Gallery Chemould in 1989. Gieve concluded the text with the image of a horizontal line in one of Atul's paintings, likening it to a note in a dhrupad recital, a minimal gesture reverberating in space, its perfect calibration altering its surroundings irrevocably. Gieve's own remarks, whether in speculative or in emphatic key, would often cast a similar spell on a conversation.

Another moment comes back to mind, bringing with it the memory of Gieve's impish, explosive laughter: some years ago, on reading the last of the essays gathered here, he called me to share his thoughts. He enjoyed my reading and contextualization of his recent paintings—and told me that he was absolutely delighted that I had, as he put it, 'caught on to my misanthropy!' I had argued that, in a series of portraits he had been developing, it was possible to detect a tension between his manifest and more empathetic attitude towards other human beings and a less evident 'misanthropic impulse, alert to the foibles of the precariously perched survivor, asserting itself through gentle, carnivalesque mockery'. His compassion for his vulnerable fellow denizens of this planet was abundant—the maimed, the eccentric, the diminished often claimed his attention—yet he could also, on occasion, regard the vexed and circum-stance-baffled human animal with dispassion, knowing well that the line between pity and self-pity can be blurred easily. The relay between these impulses imparted a robust emotional gravitas to his paintings.

*

Somewhat unusually in a field as vehemently secularized as the con-temporary arts, Gieve and I shared an abiding preoccupation with the life of spiritual quest—not as an academic interest or a research topic, but as an existential reality. He had worked on his translation of the seventeenth-century Gujarati mystic Akho's poetry for five decades (included in his *Collected Poems*, 2017); I worked on the fourteenth-century Kashmiri mystic Lal Ded's poetry for two decades (it appeared as *I, Lalla: The Poems of Lal Ded*, 2011). At a crucial moment in his life, Gieve had found anchorage at the Mirtola Ashram, a Vaishnava retreat established in the Himalayan foothills of Uttarakhand by Sri Yashoda Mai (née Monica Roy) and Sri Krishna Prem (born Ronald Henry Nixon), and headed, at the time of Gieve's visits there, by Sri Madhava Ashish (born Alexander Phipps).

My own pluralist journey has led me, variously, to profoundly replenishing meetings with Swami Niranjanananda Saraswati of the Bihar School of Yoga and Dhammachari Lokamitra (born Jeremy Goody) of the Jivaka Centre; to lifelong engagements with Kashmir Shaiva practice and the Yogāchāra school of Mahayana Buddhism. I served, from 1996 to 1999, as the *Times of India*'s first Religion & Philosophy Editor. Both Gieve and I were struck by the fact that, although a number of modernists were dedicated to the spiritual quest and even to outright religious affiliations—among others, Kandinsky and Mondrian were Theosophists, Mark Tobey was a Baha'i—the general tendency in the art world has been to regard the spiritual orientation and the religious imagination with scepticism. For Gieve and for me, it was important to secure a zone of reflection and inquiry into these subjects, away from the twin pressures of aggressive secularization on the one hand and politicized religiosity on the other, each as dogmatic, reductive, intolerant and ultimately unproductive as the other.

What Gieve and I had in common in this sphere, above all, was our shared preoccupation with the thought of J. Krishnamurti. Although K, as he was referred to by the circle around him, would have disclaimed the notion of 'thought', given his fundamental assertion that one must arrive at the cessation of thought with all its restless, comparative tendencies and its binaristic, polarizing effects—which, in turn, would mark the renunciation of the ego and one's sense of finitude in time, and could bring about a genuine freedom in the recognition of one's interrelationship to all created beings and things.

Gieve and I had arrived at Krishnamurti by different routes. I had come to him through a family connection with Theosophy, with two great-uncles who had been members of the circle around Krishnamurti's first mentor, Annie Besant. When Krishnamurti broke with Theosophy and rejected the messianic future that had been planned for him, they went with him, collaborating on the educational initiative, premised on creativity and experiment, which would bear fruit in the Krishnamurti schools at Rajghat in Banaras, Rishi Valley near Madanapalle, and Brockwood Park in Hampshire. Gieve came to K through his search for a space and a language in which he could explore his wonderment at what lies beyond without being conscripted into an unquestioning devotionalism or a scripted path. For both of us, K was that rare spiritual teacher who emphasized beauty as a value in itself, and indeed as a replenishing horizon of being, a path to wholeness.

Thus began, for Gieve, a long-term commitment to the Krishnamurti Foundation's school at Rishi Valley: every year, from 1994 until quite recently, he would be the writer-in-residence at the school, holding an annual poetry workshop for the students. Accomplished work emerged from this workshop, with a number of the students honing their literary abilities and all of them being transformed by the experience; eventually, an anthology of poems selected from several generations of Gieve's Rishi Valley students was published by the Sahitya Akademi, India's National Academy of Letters.

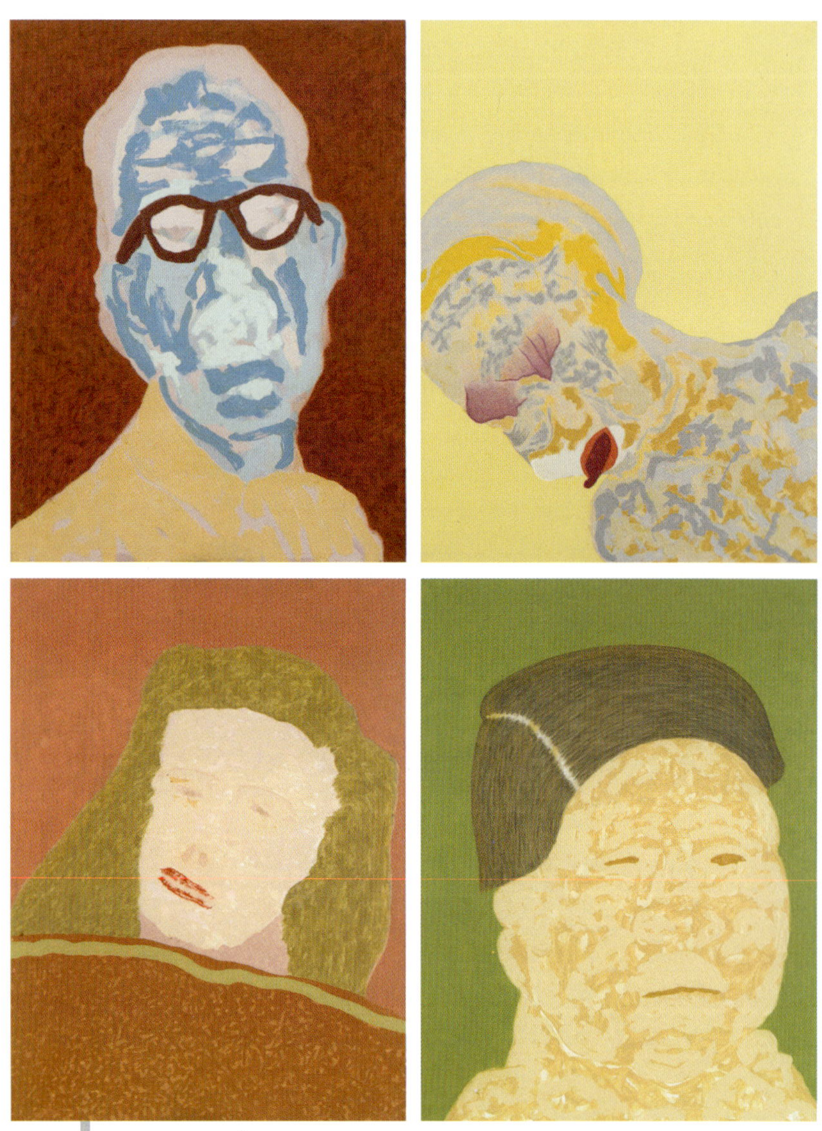

MEDITATIONS ON OLD AGE, 1–4 (2013)

Gieve's investment in the spiritual dimension of life explains, perhaps, the dynamic brushwork, the manner of handling pigment that he evolved during the late phase of his artistic career. It allowed him to embrace figures and landscapes, trees and water bodies, animals and birds into a polyphonic unity. In such paintings as *Looking into a Well: A Spray of Blossoms* or the series titled *Meditations on Old Age*, we feel the throb of a universal vitality, an unambiguous and palpable thingness that connects diverse orders of being across varied scales of time ranging from the ephemeral to the perennial.

*

As I come to the end of this introduction, I realize—with binding finality, really, for the first time since Gieve's passing—that there will be no more studio visits to Malabar Apartments or Cusrow Baug, no more walks around the Hanging Gardens, no more conversations with Nancy and me, the exchanges punctuated with laughter and delectable Parsi Gujarati phrases. Our gentle ritual of lifting a large painting from the floor to the easel, each of us matching the other's pace and pressure, resting it on dowel pins at the appropriate height, then stepping back to observe the surface with its shifting balance between detail and scale, to be startled by the bold colour combinations or comforted by the pensive palette—none of this will take place in life now; only in the re-runs that memory enacts.

The essays that follow were all written in the afterglow of such encounters with Gieve's work. My attempt, in each of them, was to bear witness both to the blood-quickening viscerality of the act of viewing and to the processes of contemplation that it generates. My attempt, also, was to chart the artist's flight path: the urgencies on which he had at various points focused his energy, the debates in which his images found their contours, the histories in which his oeuvre could find habitation. For myself, I shall always revisit Gieve Patel's work and savour the ways in which it will continue to disclose aspects of itself; and I shall cherish the memory of the years we had with him. This book is an offering in remembrance.

Bombay
Christmas Day 2023

1.

An Economy of Violence

Gieve Patel is not one of those painters who evade the grief, violence and affliction of their society by resorting to elaborate symbolism. Over the years, he has chosen to document the disasters rather than the much-publicized triumphs of humankind's evolutionary march, gathering his reports together into a subversive *Gallery of Man*. This series of anti-portraits, which oscillates between the ironic and the elegiac in tone, includes a dead politician lying in state, smothered in flowers; a drowned woman; a leper; a eunuch; and a man whose head has been crushed in a truck accident. And yet Patel is also a healer: his compassionate treatment confers a tragic dignity upon those who are not blessed with grace—the wounded, the maimed, the disfigured and the dead—redeeming them from their turbulent environment. Increasingly, too, Patel has begun to explore a contemplative idiom of painting that enables him to pass from the realm of necessity, the bondage of social relationships and political structures, to a realm of freedom glimpsed in the soaring flight of a bird over a pond, or in the deep shaft of a well.

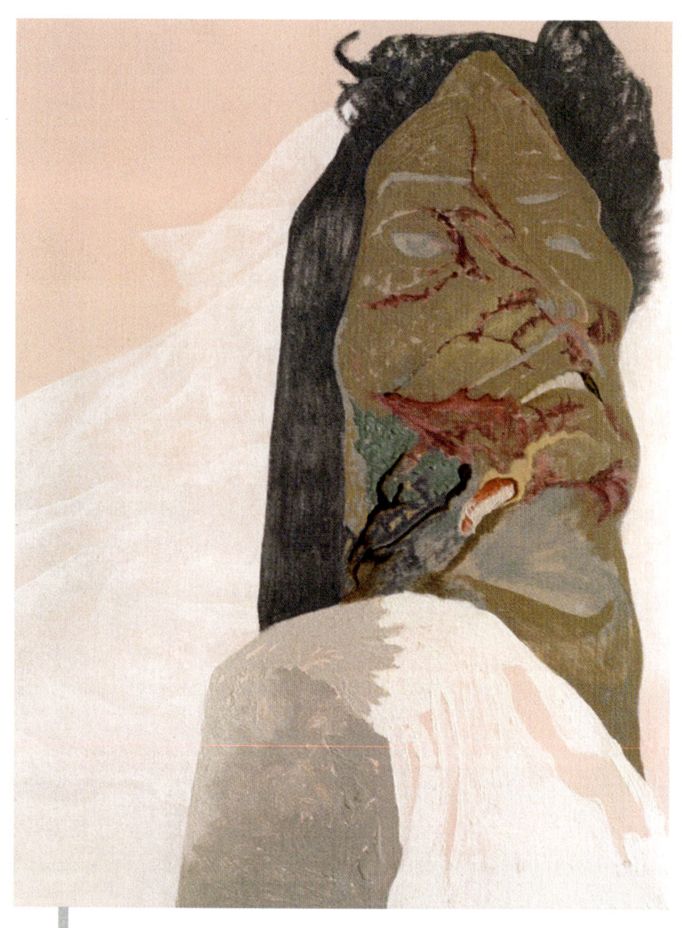

CRUSHED HEAD (1984)

DROWNED WOMAN (1984)

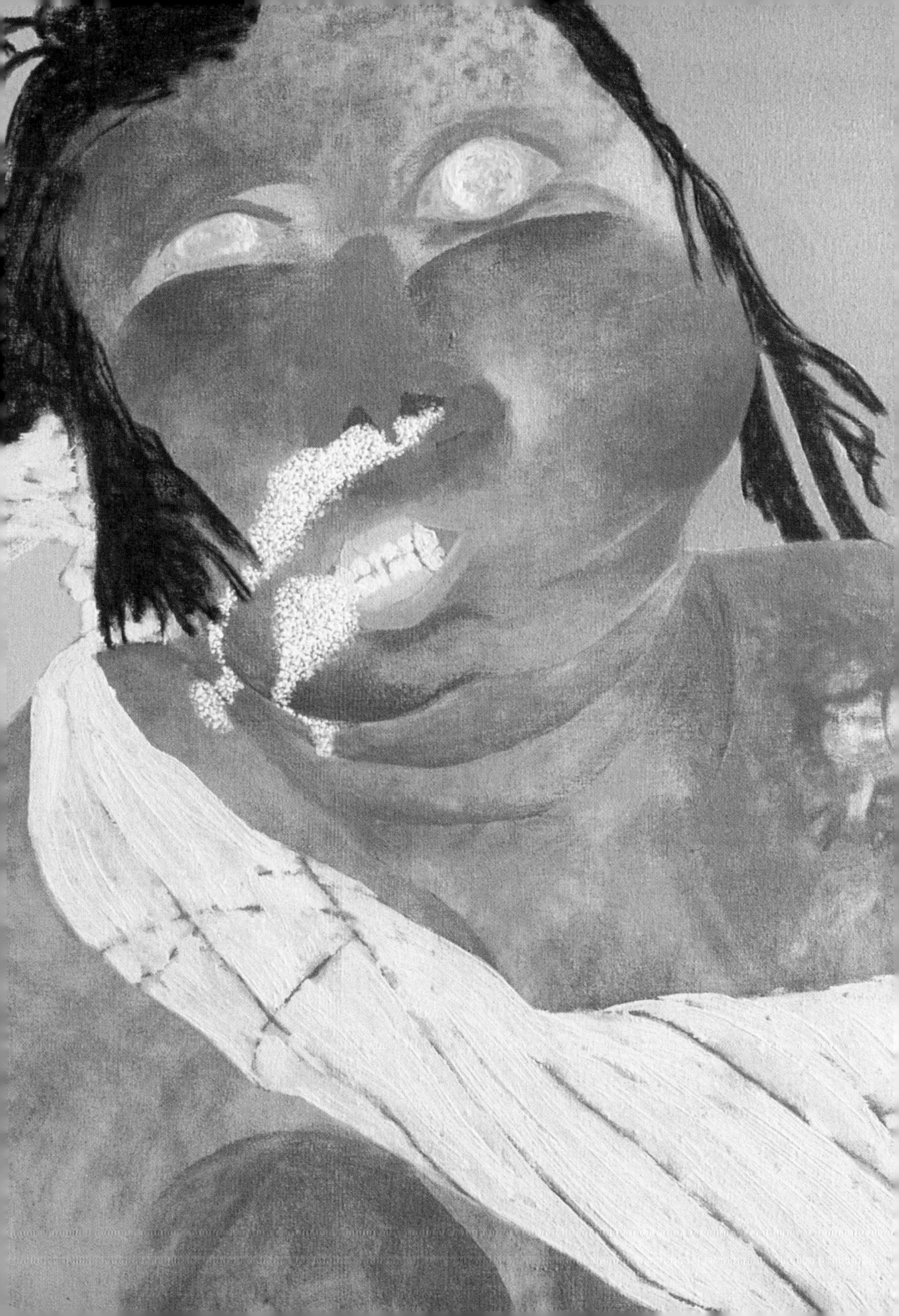

Since 1966, when he held his first exhibition, Patel has amplified on these themes, elaborating them along a spectrum that stretches from horror at the brutal pathology of everyday life on the one hand, to wonder at the possibilities of transcendence on the other. In the present exhibition, the artist invites us to consider eight recent canvases, each embodying a particular phase of his development, a pattern of mutations and resonances mapped across the 34 years he has devoted to painting. Taken together, these eight works testify to a major shift in Patel's evolving preoccupation with the nature of violence. From the 1960s through the 1980s, Patel remained engaged with the intensity of direct violence as enacted upon the human body; his paintings often took the form of a close-up presentation of evidence. By the 1990s, though, he had begun to situate the portrait of the assault victim in a larger context. *Battered Man in a Landscape* (1993), for instance, displays a grotesquely mutilated corpse abandoned on a beach—not in theatrical close-up, but bracketed within an armature of bleached strand and farther ocean. The artist had stripped off his romantic taste for catastrophe and modulated a fierce history of grief into a requiem.

Patel now examines violence that is casual or accidental rather than premeditated. His paintings are no longer a presentation of evidence, but studies of an economy of violence: the emphasis has moved to the witnesses and beneficiaries, the secondary, incidental figures who profit from violence without having been the inquisitors or executioners who set it in motion in the first place. Patel's new works constitute an expression of amazement at the riddle of inexplicable suffering, at the cosmic injustice by which one individual's tragedy can translate as another's advantage. The four eponymous birds in *Crows* (1999), scavengers feasting on a dead rat splayed on the ground with its innards spilling out, symbolize this situation. So, too, do the crows settling down to pick at a rat sliced in half

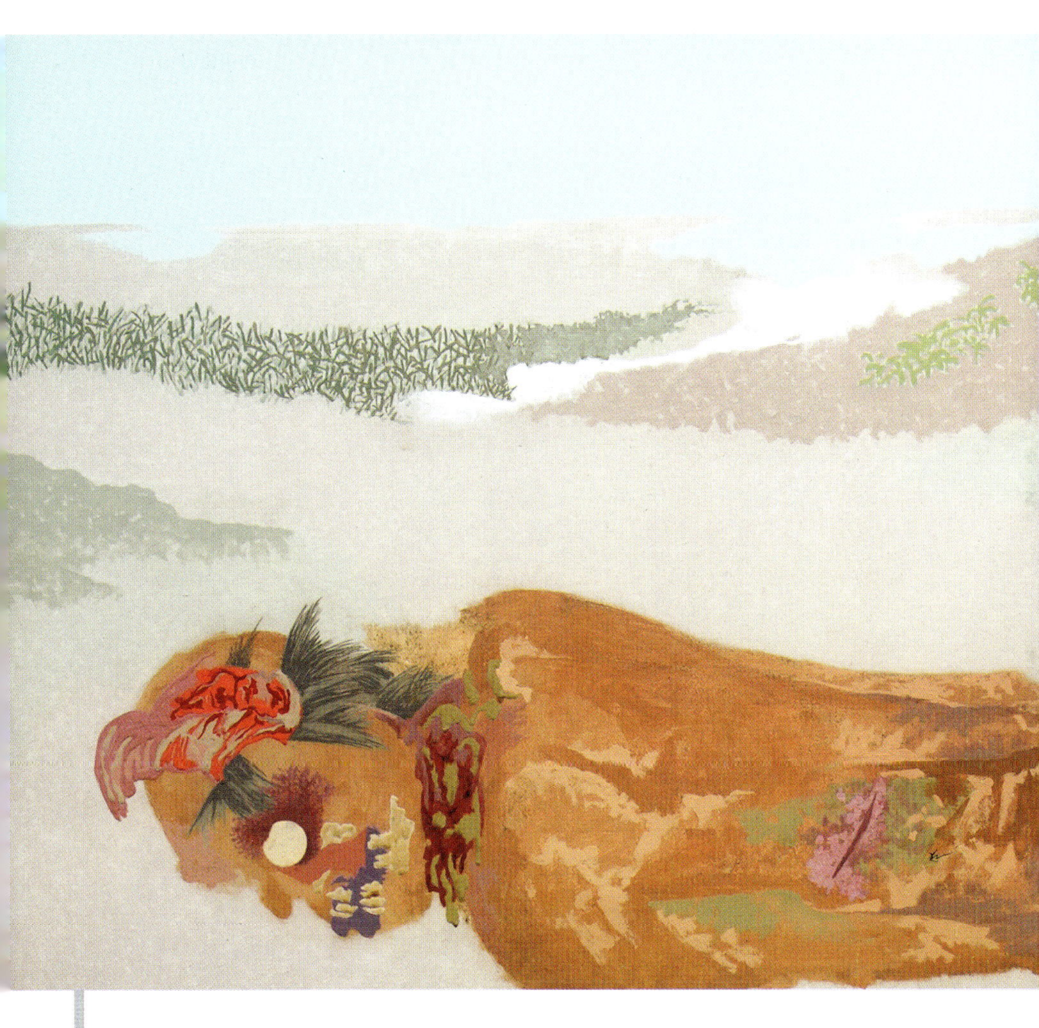

BATTERED MAN IN A LANDSCAPE (1993)

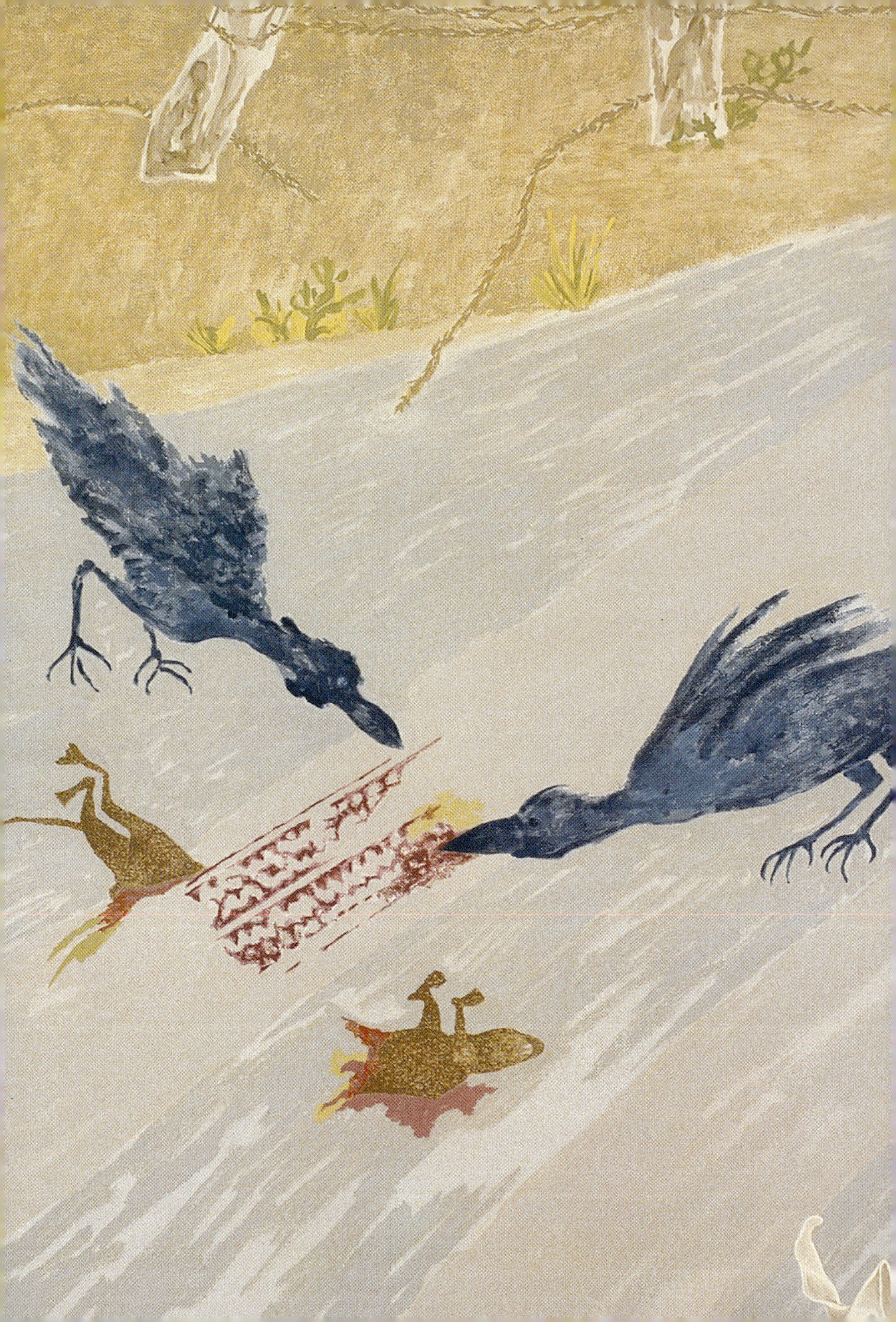

by a passing car in *Crows with Debris* (1999). The former painting captures a simple ecological rite of cleansing that may strike us as callous, but is efficient; moreover, knowing the crows' own lowly place in the hierarchy of being, it occurs to us that victim and victimizer are fairly interchangeable here, snared within the same Darwinian natural history as they are. The latter painting forces us to stare at the fatal tyre-tread, a used condom and a fence topped by broken barbed wire: the transience of pleasure and the abortion of quest are annotated, as it were, in a piquant stenography.

Patel views birds and animals as creatures caught up in a complex structure of relationships and transactions with humankind—as fellow sentient beings, sharers of fate, heraldic symbols, instinctive predators and inarticulate victims—and they have played no small role in his art. The principal philosophical source of inspiration for the crow paintings is a passage from the *Taittiriya Upanishad* that has long captivated Patel; it visualizes the world as a vast and perpetual food cycle, self-cannibalistic and self-renewing, a looped and nested hierarchy of eaters and eaten linked together by the unvoiced logic of slaughter. Patel's crows are not strictly ornithological specimens, but they are not caricatures either. Protagonists in an anti-pastoral, their body language is distinctive: with their expressionistically rendered beaks, wings and claws, they embody the hunger of the marginalized, who must practise a cynical opportunism, perfect an indifference to injustice and grief in order to survive.

II.

The issue of body language brings us to another of Patel's continuing preoccupations: the working-class or vagrant figure cast in its local and immediate lifeworld, a figure that undergoes the crippling strain of hard labour or social stigma and yet endures. Through portraits drawn from the proletarian, the dispossessed and the marginal populations—construction workers, porters navigating the platforms of deserted railway stations, lunatics, derelicts, rag-pickers and beggars—Patel has sought to confront the inequities of postcolonial Indian society, to expose its institutionalized forms of oppression, exploitation and stigmatization. From the 1960s through the 1990s, Patel's figurative concerns ran in parallel with those of his younger confrere Sudhir Patwardhan: both painters treasured the ideal of corporal resilience and saw themselves as responsible spokespersons for the subaltern classes; but while Patwardhan mobilized a heroic proletarian body that could expand to internalize the stresses acting on it, Patel constructed a more yielding physique, one that would suffer the distortions of shock, trauma and disease, yet stubbornly refuse the label of 'victim'.

Langra Mangoes (1998) is set in the main avenue of Bombay's colonial quarter, the Fort. Painted as a stippled massif, the neo-Gothic High Court building forms a backdrop that resembles a mountain range rather than an architectural edifice; subliminally, this conveys the rural origins of the people who occupy the street in the foreground—a woman in a yellow sari, a mango vendor and a boy eating a mango that burns orange and green in his hand. The boy's body bears the characteristic signs of want; the umbrella hooked on his shoulder looks, at first sight, like a freak limb. Patel has always accentuated the hideous in his paintings: his figures are not just ungainly, they actively challenge our canon of taste with their protruding teeth, hunched shoulders, uneven features, rickety frames and tubercular fingers. Through the years, Patel has introduced us to a repertory of such memorable characters, including the garland-crowned madman in the street, the child narrowly rescued from a hypnotic fire,

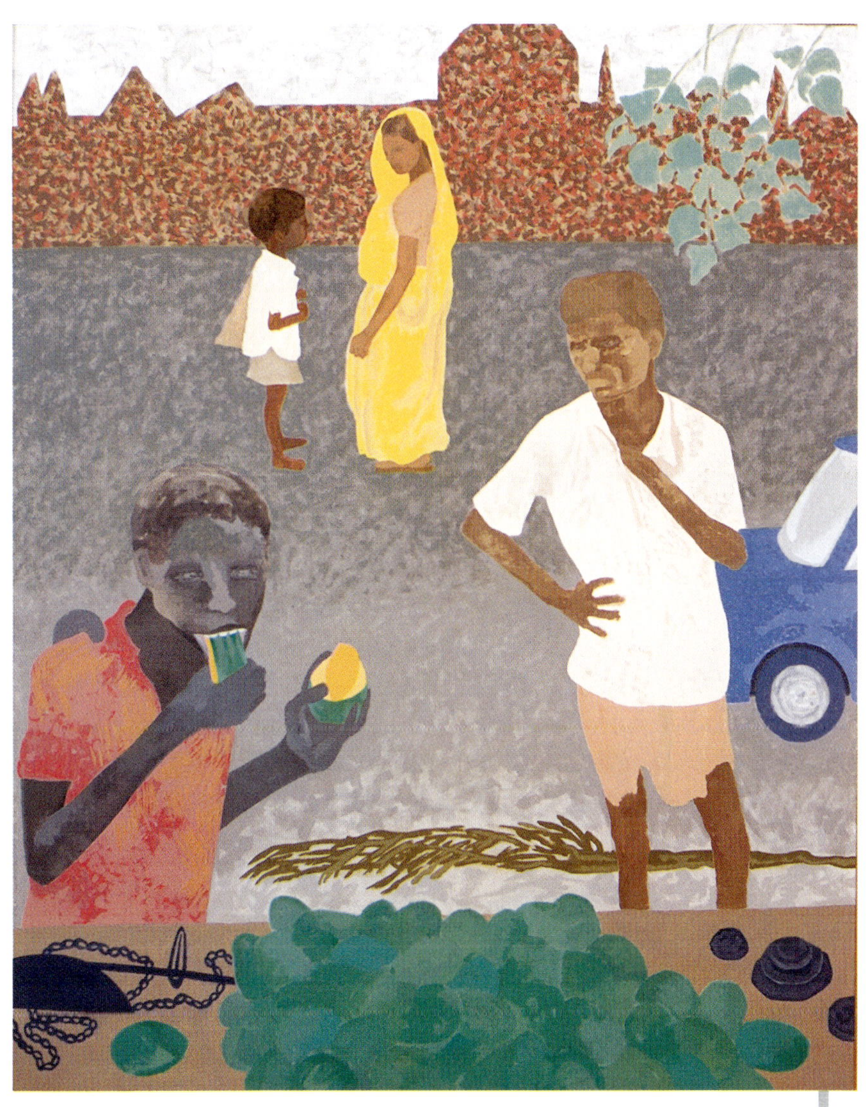

LANGRA MANGOES (1998)

the tattered scarecrow of a man holding on to his umbrella and a trove of bananas in pouring rain.

Patel has deliberately adopted the anti-heroic figuration of teratology, the science of monsters, because its vocabulary of ugliness contests our aesthetic assumptions. We are unnerved by atrophy and amputation, which are lack; by hypertrophy and excrescence, which are excess. By deviating from our ideal norms, Patel's protagonists call our conventional apparatus of organic form and symmetry, pleasure and supple grace into question. If Patel's figures verge on the grotesque, the grotesquerie is drawn from the reality of our tropical streets and postcolonial shanties—in reacting to them with trepidation, we become sensitized to the social and economic conditions that have produced them, to the malnutrition, starvation, ethnic discrimination and thwarted opportunities that they incarnate in their stunted or malformed appearance.

In *Stroll* (1997), which is woven around the relationship between a girl-child and a man, Patel participates in the private drama of the sub-altern classes. The father seems burdened by loss, but his playful daughter is oblivious to the conspiracies of history—like a little miracle, a Virgin from a Goan or Mexican fiesta, she personifies the perennial hope of renewal, the fortitude with which the oppressed defy the forces of destiny. Patel cites Ritwik Ghatak's cinematic masterpiece, *Subarnarekha*, as a trigger for the abiding image of the child leading the adult, but the image has an ancestry in Patel's own work, especially in *Near the Bus Stop* (1991), a painting in which a girl feeds an armless beggar. Formally, *Stroll* allows Patel to delight in an interplay between the diaphanous material of the girl's bonnet and the peeling, moss-covered walls of the tall buildings in the background. These details of architectural decrepitude have long fascinated the artist, and take their place within his broader interest in the cityscape, where the success or failure of built form shapes the basic

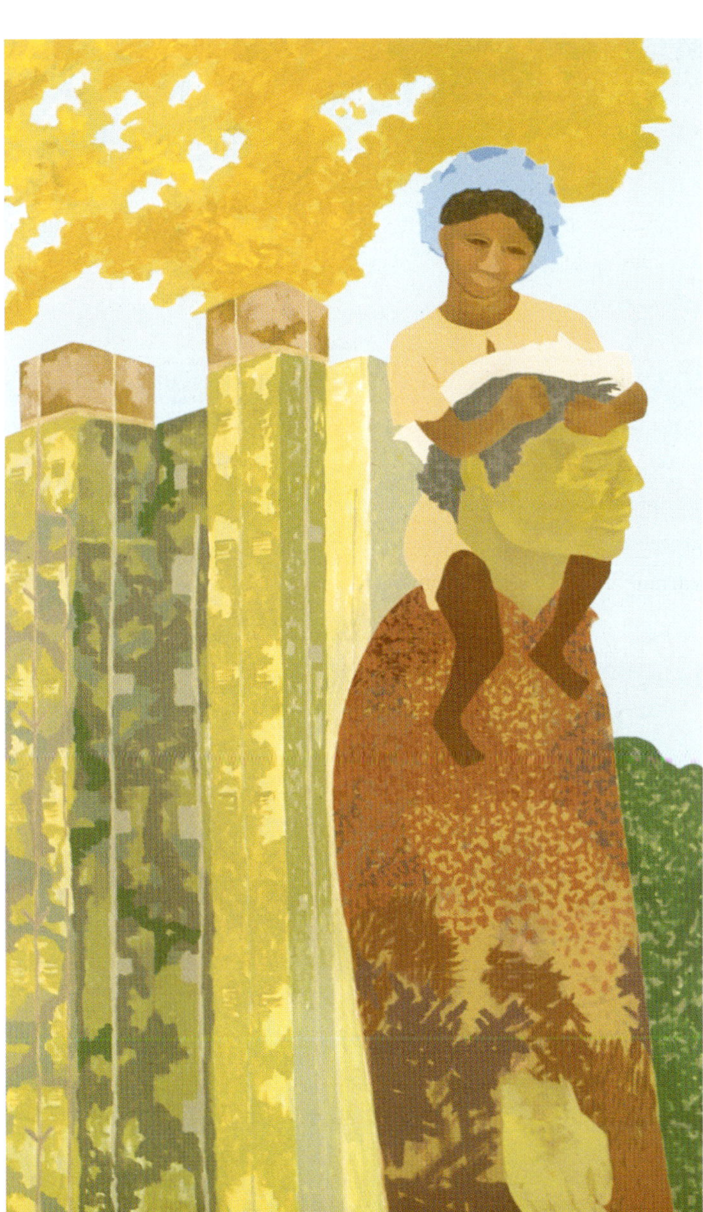

STROLL
(1997)

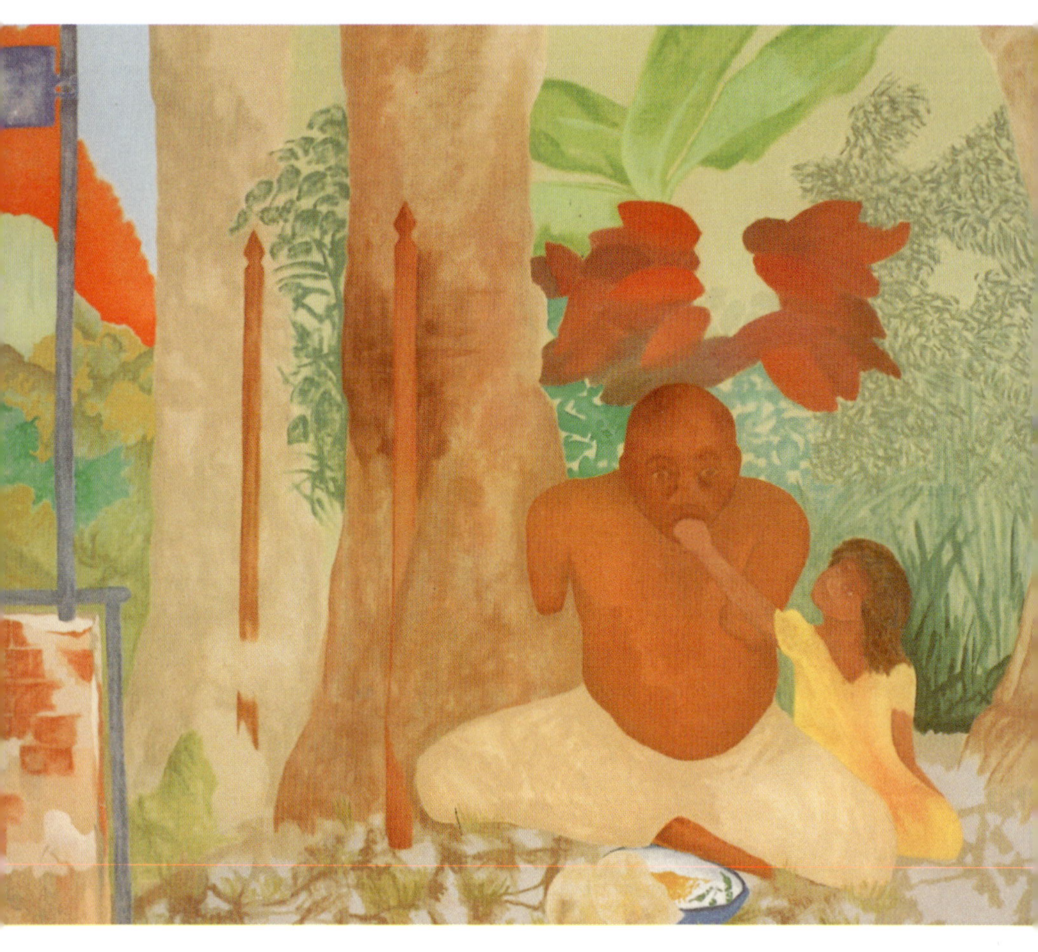

NEAR THE BUS STOP (1991)

environment. In the 1979 painting, *Two Men with A Handcart*, for example, Patel provides testimony to the monumentality of urban architecture, while also subtly underscoring the exclusion of the brick-layers from their own creation.

III.

Over the last decade, Patel's paintings have gradually relinquished their taut focus on social reality; the artist's philosophical investigations have led him back to the primal sources of replenishment, to the gnarled trunk of the banyan and the origin of water. Patel has gravitated, since 1991, towards the central image of the well: it promises to reflect us when we look in, but the reflection is shot through with other presences; looking into its shaft, we find ourselves about to plunge into an epiphanic tunnel of rebirth. The ongoing *Wells* series is represented by *Brimming Well, Dipping Fronds* (1993), which conveys the synapse that takes place when a banana tree bends to touch the tapestries of algae floating on the water, and *Looking into a Well* (1999), with its mirror image of a sunburst exploding behind a date palm. Patel has addressed himself to two technical problems in the execution of his wells—first, that of painting water, a material that is both reflecting surface and deep substance; and second, that of avoiding the classic perspective-hole method of rendering a well (which the artist regards as melodramatic), while nevertheless producing a sensation of depth. In the process of memorializing the well as an interface between the everyday and the miraculous, Patel has granted himself the freedom to develop a new formal language: his open handling of texture indicates a move towards lyric abstraction, which may seem to be an appropriate means of expressing the transcendental impulse.

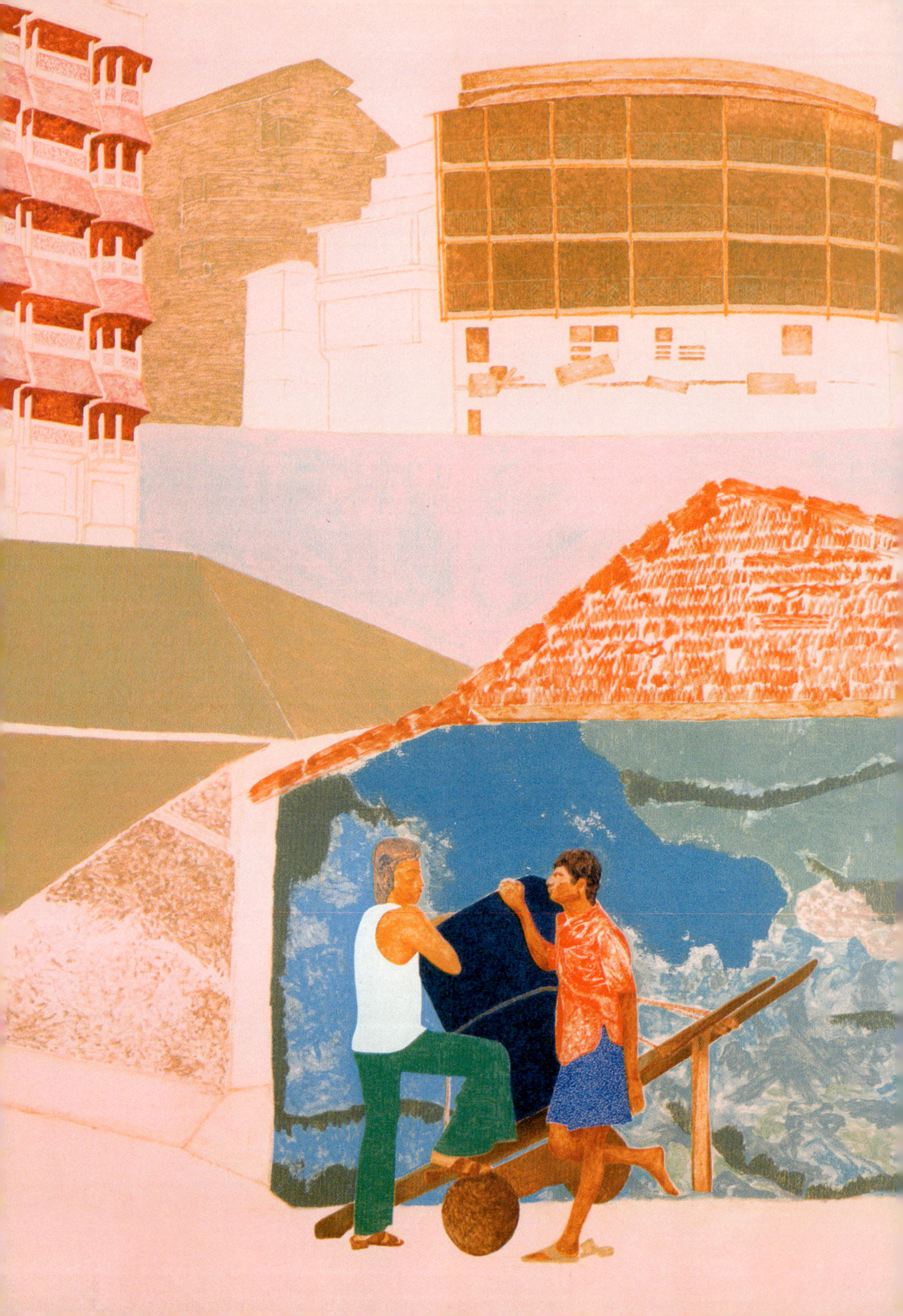

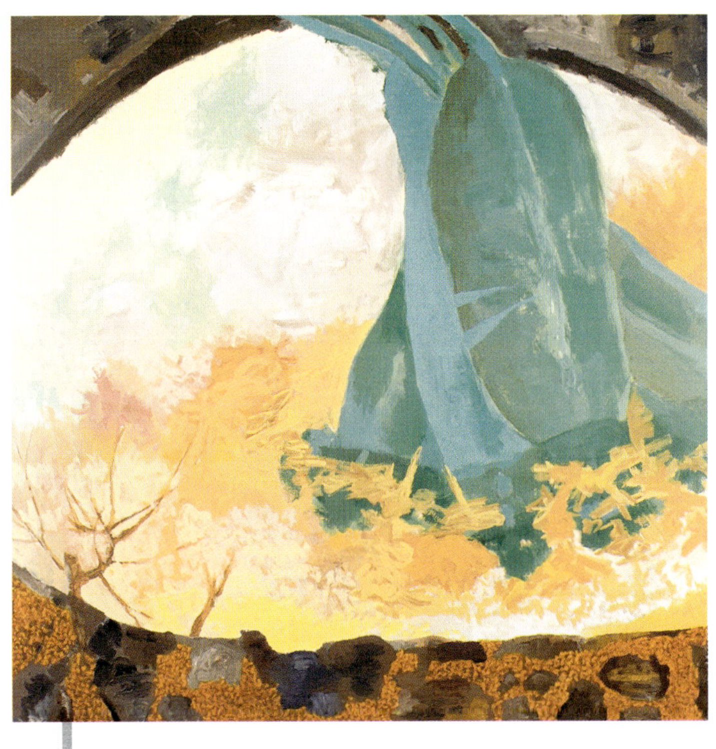

BRIMMING WELL, DIPPING FRONDS (1993)

TWO MEN WITH A HANDCART (1979)

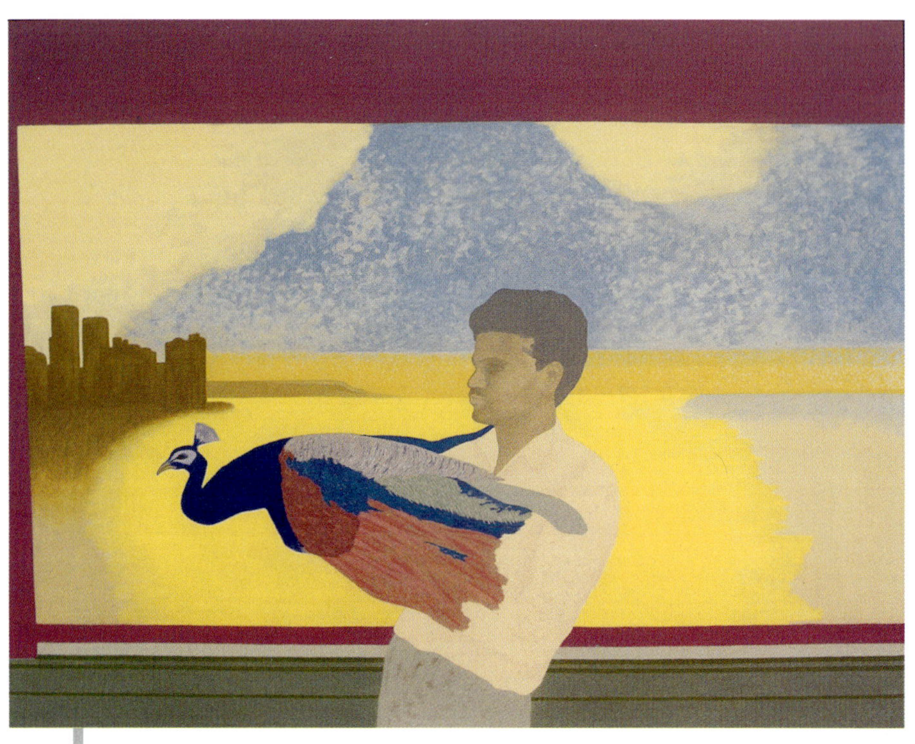

PEACOCK AT NARIMAN POINT (1999)

Significantly, however, the transcendental impulse is best symbolized in this exhibition, not by a semi-abstractionist image, but by a very concrete one—*Peacock at Nariman Point* (1999). This is the latest in a line of magical birds that Patel invokes to surprise the viewer into a moment of heightened awareness, the other two being the giant parrot descending from the sky in the celebrated *Off Lamington Road* (1982–86) and the white bird slashing diagonally across a sun-burned pond in *The Water Tank at Nargol* (1993). Indeed, this exhibition stages a counterpoint between two bird paintings that are completely opposed in mood and intent, *Peacock at Nariman Point* and *Crow with Egg-shell* (1999). A word, first, about the latter, which is a portrait of the crow as nihilist: holding an egg-shell in its beak like a trophy of war, it partakes of the manic, primeval quality of Ted Hughes' Crow to some degree. The egg is a symbol of fertility, and this painting could be read as an allegory of the imagination under threat from destructive forces.

Peacock at Nariman Point, by contrast, is a festival in mauve and yellow—a man holds up a peacock against the severe geometry of a corporate office. The genesis of this painting lies in a compelling photograph by Hoshi Jal, which appeared in the Times of India some years ago, of a peacock that had strayed from Malabar Hill to Nariman Point, the business and government hub of Bombay. The image gave Patel the opportunity to paint that delicious incongruity, a legendary creature framed against the skyscrapers and tower-blocks of the South Bombay skyline. Without the newspaper report to moor it in a specific context, the photograph becomes intriguing, inexplicable; as the found image gathers coherence, Patel works out the relation between man and bird. The frame becomes incandescent with the sense of restrained energy, as though a resplendent spirit were attempting to leap out from an earth-anchored body.

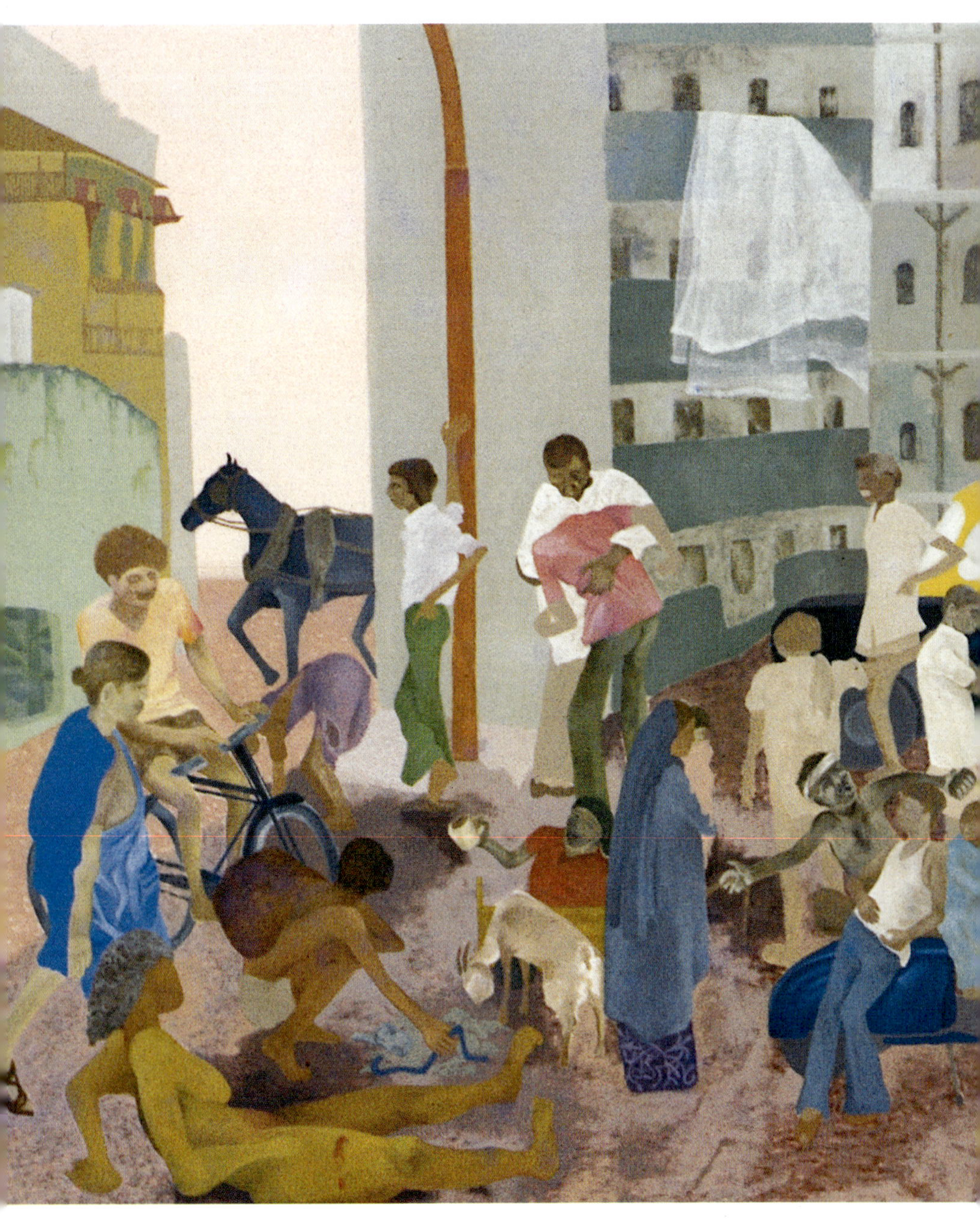

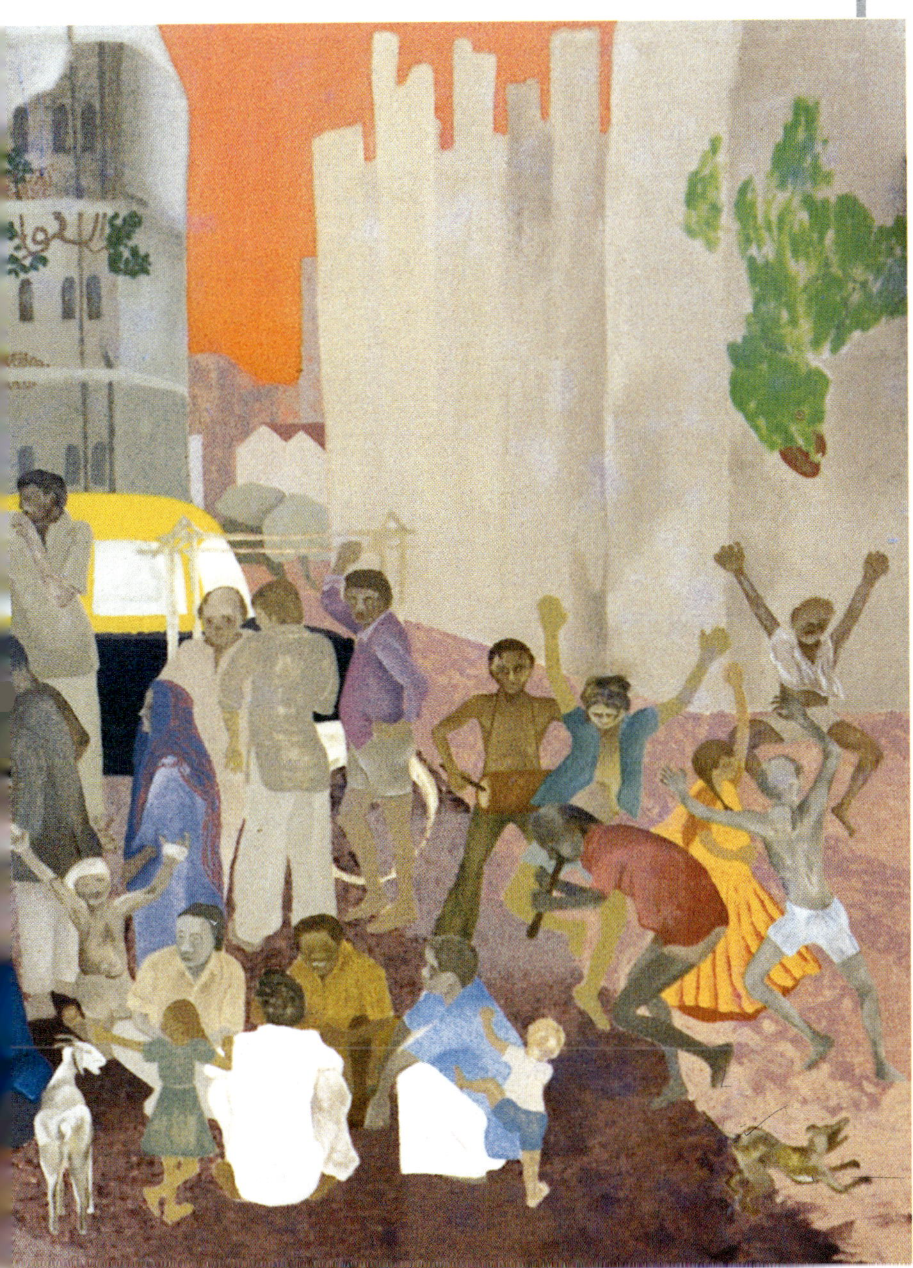

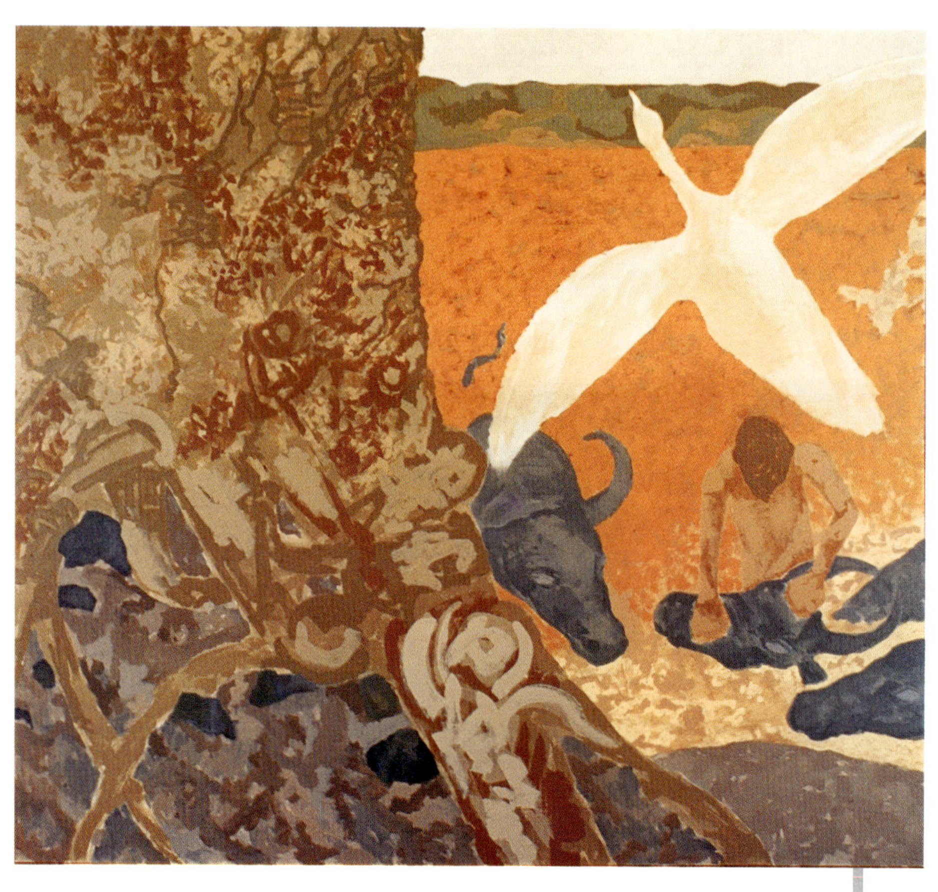

THE WATER TANK AT NARGOL (1993)

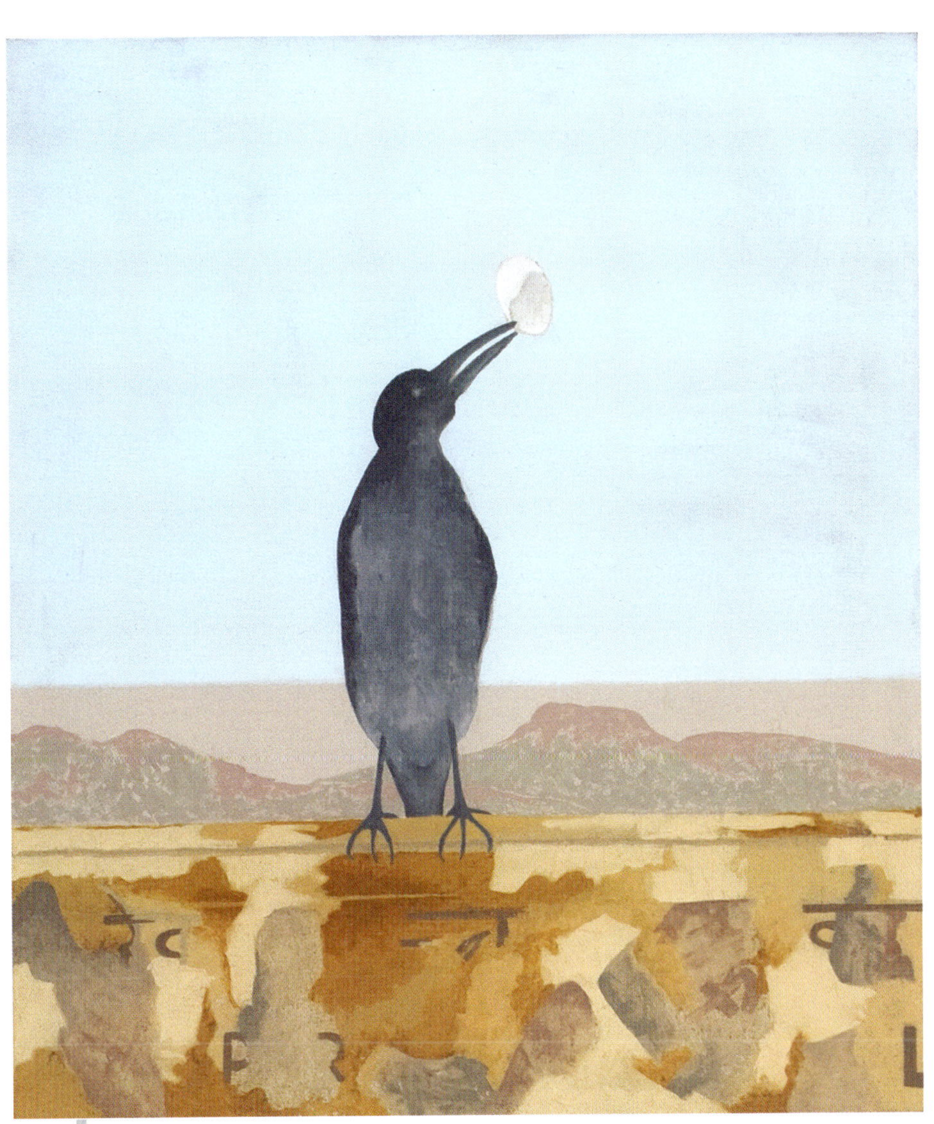

CROW WITH EGG-SHELL (1999)

Patel's art may aspire to a transcendence, but it does not disdain the earth. Indeed, it infuses the breath of the transcendent into people and objects by first gathering them into a common materiality of daubs and splashes, a structural unity suggestive of a shared predicament, and a shared possibility of overcoming it. If the artist subscribes to a humanism, it is not that large and ultimately vaporous humanism of statement which has so signally failed to effect communion between the human and natural worlds. His is, rather, an inclusive humanism that acknowledges the secret vitality lodged in every tangled root, leprous rock and rough-ridden beast. Gieve Patel meditates on the calloused hands of reality; and with those hands, he grasps a rope and lowers a pail into the waters of renewal.

Bombay
February 2000

2.

The Incarnate Particularity of Forms

GIEVE PATEL, PAINTINGS 2001–2003

The windows of Gieve Patel's studio open on a many-birded peepal tree, a branching refuge, not only for crows, mynahs and sun-birds, but also for golden orioles, coppersmiths, the occasional kingfisher and, through the summer, parakeets. Beyond the tree, a path slopes up a hill; once a muddy track, now tamed by flagstones, it winds past a washerwomen's pool and passes under a spreading banyan before it reaches the garden on the crest of the hill. Just over the rise, but unsuspected from the studio, Bombay's traffic screeches and roars, the purpose of its movement lost to the performance. Patel has long been preoccupied with the manner in which the rural and the urban encounter and modify each other in the postcolonial Indian experience. As a child, he spent his schooldays in Bombay, his vacations in Nargol; as a young physician, he elected to work at a primary health centre in the village of Sanjan, before returning to the metropolis. In the early poem, 'Nargol' (from *Poems*, 1966), he recalls how, on periodic visits to his ancestral village in coastal Gujarat, he is accosted by a beggar woman who regards him as privileged, not only by reason of family prestige and education, but also by his status as a Bombay man who rarely comes back; each visit must be gilded by largesse. The burden being oppressive in several ways, Patel writes: 'Walking to the sea I carry / A village, a city, the country, / For the moment / On my back.'

The beggar's claim on the returning native activates the self-doubt of the individual in transit between two conditions. If Patel's poetry has been haunted by the burden that the individual suffers, when a shift of frame produces a shift in others' perception of him—their reading of his social location and existential purpose, their imposition of an identity upon him—his painting stands back from the personal immediacy of this predicament. As in this recent suite of paintings, executed over 2001–2003, Patel's eye dwells on the terrain within which this drama is staged; he presents us, not with a neat dichotomy of urban and rural, but with an interpenetration of the two. In the three paintings in the present exhibition that have been developed around figures, the protocols of the urban manifest themselves in the rural; the reflexes of the rural persist within the urban. Patel offers us a range of dramatis personae from the margins of metropolitan life: a man in the rain; a scribe and his client; and a madman. Under the focus of Patel's gaze, they emerge from their marginality to command our attention as vital presences. All four characters are shown to be occupying public space, but performing acts that lie in an intermediate zone between the private and the public; for these figures are survivors. Circumstances have carried them far away from the territories to which, however tenuously, they belonged; they have sought a refuge in the metropolis, or have created one for themselves, with the materials and spaces available at hand, somewhat like the birds in Patel's tree.

These figurative works exemplify Patel's practice of working in series: many of his images take their place in a genealogy, a sequence of avatars that evolves from his fascination with subject matter and, I suspect, with the possibilities of an allusive narrative-by-condensation. At the same time, such recursion marks the artist's long-standing commitment to the exploration of specific formal problems of representation. From these motives spring the iconographies and situations that have held his attention over two decades, and which recur in these paintings: the large sitting figure, the figure standing with its arms akimbo, the man in the rain (and, I must add, the iconic head: at the time of writing, Patel is at work on a male head, wearing thick spectacles, apparently baffled by events, and a female head, mysterious, imbued with flame-like self-possession).

The eponymous *Man in the Rain with Bread and Bananas* (1990), for instance, makes his fourth appearance in Patel's oeuvre here. He is a membrane between isolation and society, this man who crouches beneath his umbrella, navigating by guesswork in a pitiless storm that, having engulfed houses, streets and gutters, has deprived him of his bearings. The vestiges of buildings loom up through the downpour, but the man battling the torrent, with visibility reduced to the edge of his umbrella, is excluded from their roofed warmth and terraced shelter. He is left in the street, gripping the means of his subsistence in rhizomatic fingers as he tests the road, a metropolitan Lear in the peculiarly public solitude of this contemporary heath. Patel's handling partakes of a judicious expressionism: the careful distortion of the man's face implies insecurity, that constant anticipation of disaster which underscores city life; but the man's gaze, though indicative of suffering, registers no alarm at our scrutiny. Ever the metropolitan, even in his distress, this man is unsurprised. Patel justifies the blue and purple torrents thundering down on

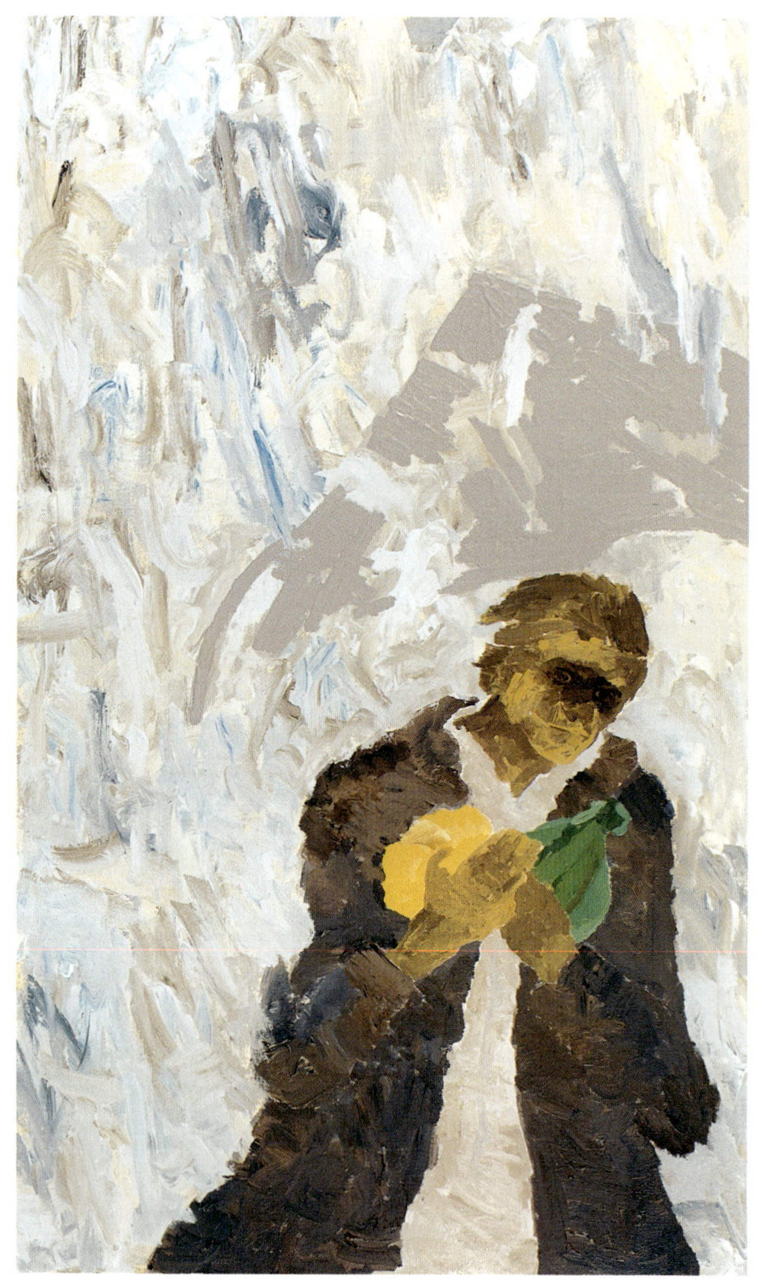

MAN IN THE RAIN WITH BREAD AND BANANAS (1990)

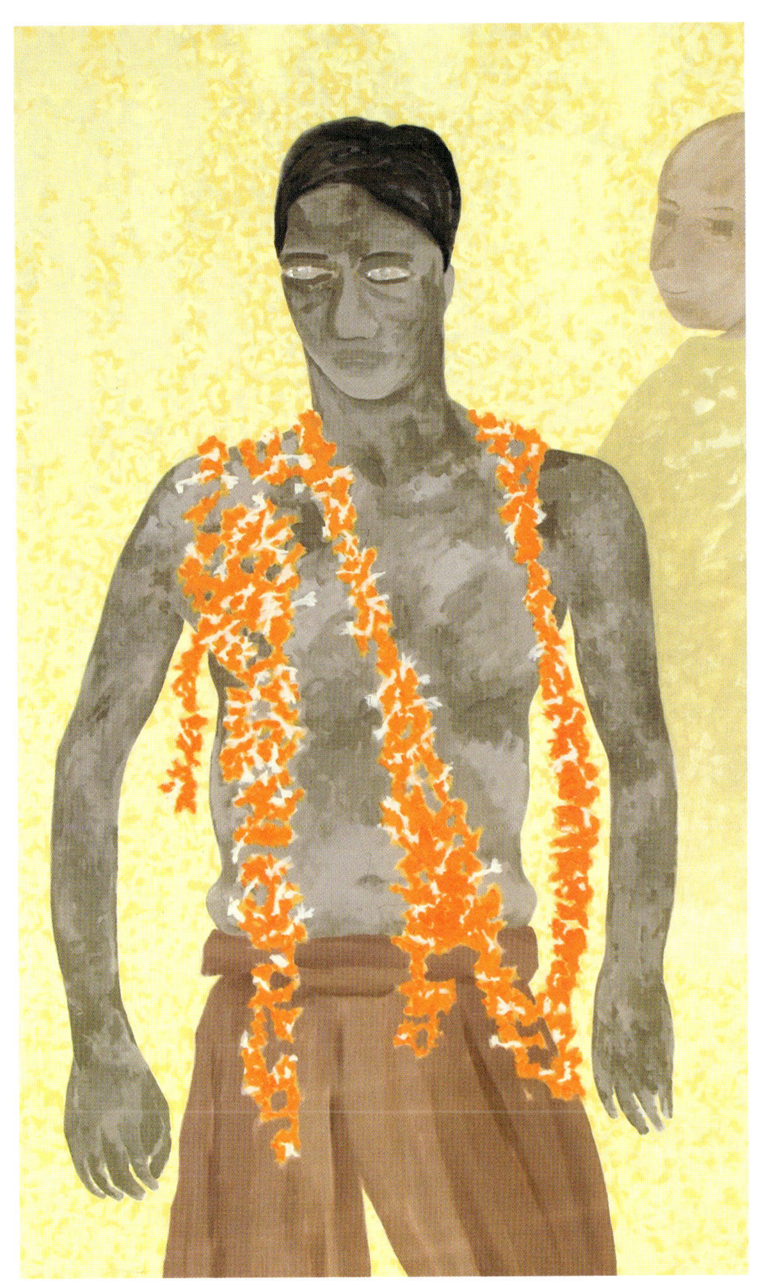

MADMAN IN THE STREET (2005)

the man's hapless umbrella, like crackers or streamers, by his ongoing exploration of the problem of how to paint water, its moods, its inconsistencies, its mutability (he takes the exploration further, in this exhibition, in his continuing *Wells* series).

In *Madman* (2003), the eponymous lunatic poses, as though for a portrait, with a public-transport BEST bus, that classic trope of the Bombay street as democratic leveller, for backdrop. Bedecked with dried flowers, the relics of a garland, he is defiant—no, nonchalant—this king of the street who ignores the passengers gawking at him from the windows of the bus. He, too, has appeared before in Patel's oeuvre: the madman as profane saint, a rural fixture easily translated into an urban milieu, offering visions to the unwary or those robotized by the daily cycle of local-train commutes and closely clocked schedules. Our appreciation of this painting is deepened by our recognition of its intertextuality, for Patel refers here to, and engages in dialogue with, two key paintings by his confrere, Sudhir Patwardhan: *The City* (1979) and *Street Play* (1981), strategically recast Bombay streetscapes that feature a BEST bus with its passengers forming a tableau in themselves while also playing audience to the main action of the painting. Indeed, in relating the lunatic-as-actor to the passengers-as-audience, *Madman* addresses a recurrent theme in Patel's art: the street as theatre, with some of the figures scripted as actors or performers and others as watchers or audience. Here, Patel catches the exact emotional pitch at which the Indian public space is transformed into a theatrical space, a drama or a circus; the provocation could be a verbal quarrel, fisticuffs, a eunuch or a policeman's display of aggression, or the mounting of a location shoot for a movie—or a madman's performance.

A related concern with the relationship between the figure and the pictorial ground above its head—as a space that could be charged with the symbolic mandate of representing the figure's thoughts or mental state—is evident in *The Letter Home* (2002). This painting is dominated by the figure of a scribe, that god of literary skills who writes letters for illiterate migrant workers in the city. The pejorative description, 'unlettered', takes on a dual nuance in this context, for the relationship between the scribe and his client is an unequal one, with authority weighted over against vulnerability. The scribe sits on a coir mat, cloud-large in his cerulean kurta and dark-blue lungi, confident; his more compactly built and modestly clothed client sits beside him, waiting upon his pauses, apparently dictating but in fact dictated to. We remark on the difference in posture and gesture, the bodies speaking more eloquently than their implied words; they sit in the shadow of a wall whose patterned surface appears to symbolize their thoughts. Beyond the wall we see a shed and a building faced in hues of green, suggestive of that quintessential Bombay combination of moss and monsoon seepage. The script tells us that the letter is being composed in Telugu; Patel's bold decision to use a Dravidian script, rather than the Latin or Devanagari scripts to which many of his viewers in western India are more accustomed, stems from several cogent reasons.

While enjoying the curlicued script as an aesthetic delight for its own sake, Patel also makes a subtle political point by acknowledging the southeastern province of Andhra Pradesh, which provides Bombay with large numbers of the construction workers who sustain its manic programme of urban development. More intimately, this is a dedication to Patel's happy association, as a visiting writer, with the Krishnamurti Foundation's progressive school at Rishi Valley, situated in that province. Having put in play the political gesture of introducing a largely 'invisible' South Indian textuality into the pictorial discourse of contemporary Indian art, Patel sets up an even subtler subversion. Freely adapting the

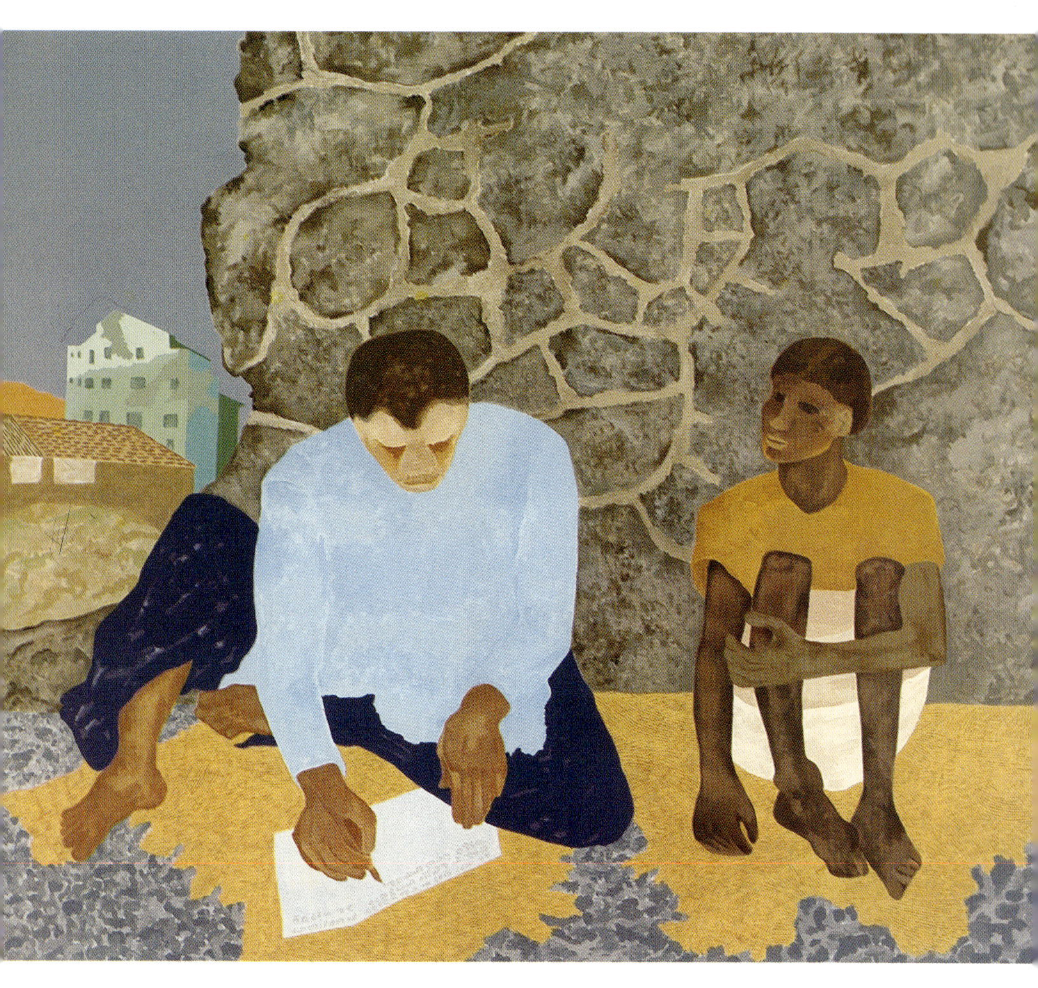

THE LETTER HOME (2002)

forms of address conventional in such letters, he deliberately mixes the idiomatic opening laid down for a letter from a husband to a wife with that signalling a letter from a son to a father. The scribal authority that determines the flow of the painting is thus cunningly undercut, as though the words had refused to obey the dictates of the pen. By discreetly questioning the scribe, Patel draws our attention to the manner in which the interpreter, that plenipotent go-between who is the natural product of transition, rules the hybrid space born of the encounter between city and village. *The Letter Home* dramatizes this space, not only through a mythology of loss and redemption, but also through the asymmetries of communication and distance, the inequalities of expertise.

In his triad of wells, which form the latest extension of a series that has been unfolding since 1991, Patel turns his attention to the envisioning of the rural in a more classical tenor: not as a social or political situation, but as a space affording contemplative repose. This must not lead us to regard the *Wells* series as being either idyllic or generic: each well is distinctive, animated, disturbing, and no less a portrait for portraying an object rather than a human being. Mirror and womb, navel of the world and tunnel into inner space, the well is a site of revelation for Patel; we find ourselves looking over the ledge into a vision of the cosmic, held in counterpoint by a miniature geography of stone, root and slime. *Looking into a Well: Full Moon* (2001) is a nocturne: a waxy moon commands a starless sky; the spectral white bulk of the wellhead and the back-lit branches are seen in reflection; or perhaps this is a view from inside the well-shaft, as framed by the mouth. *Looking into a Well: Foliage* (2002) invites us, not to gaze into the traditional well, but to consider the surface of an artesian well, its shaft bored deep into the earth; an irrigation pipe, installed to siphon water into the fields, strikes a severe note, its geometry at odds with the luxuriance of the rest of the painting, the gleam of light

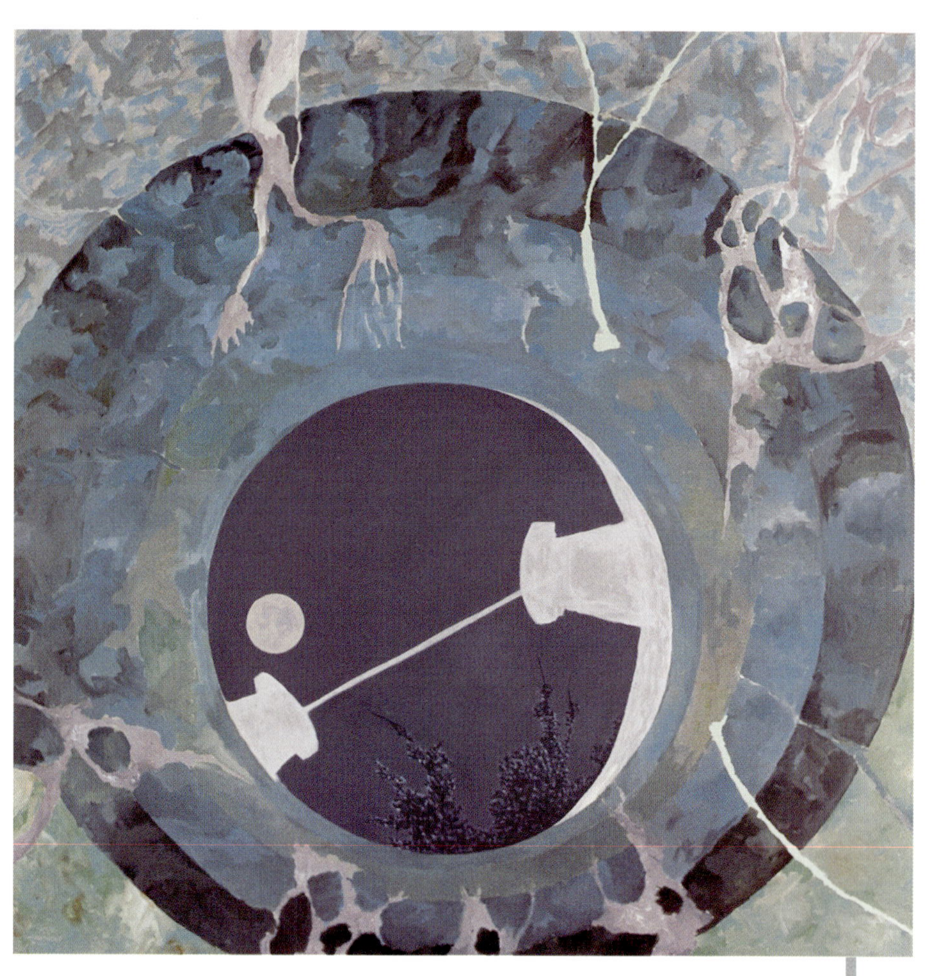

LOOKING INTO A WELL: FULL MOON (2001)

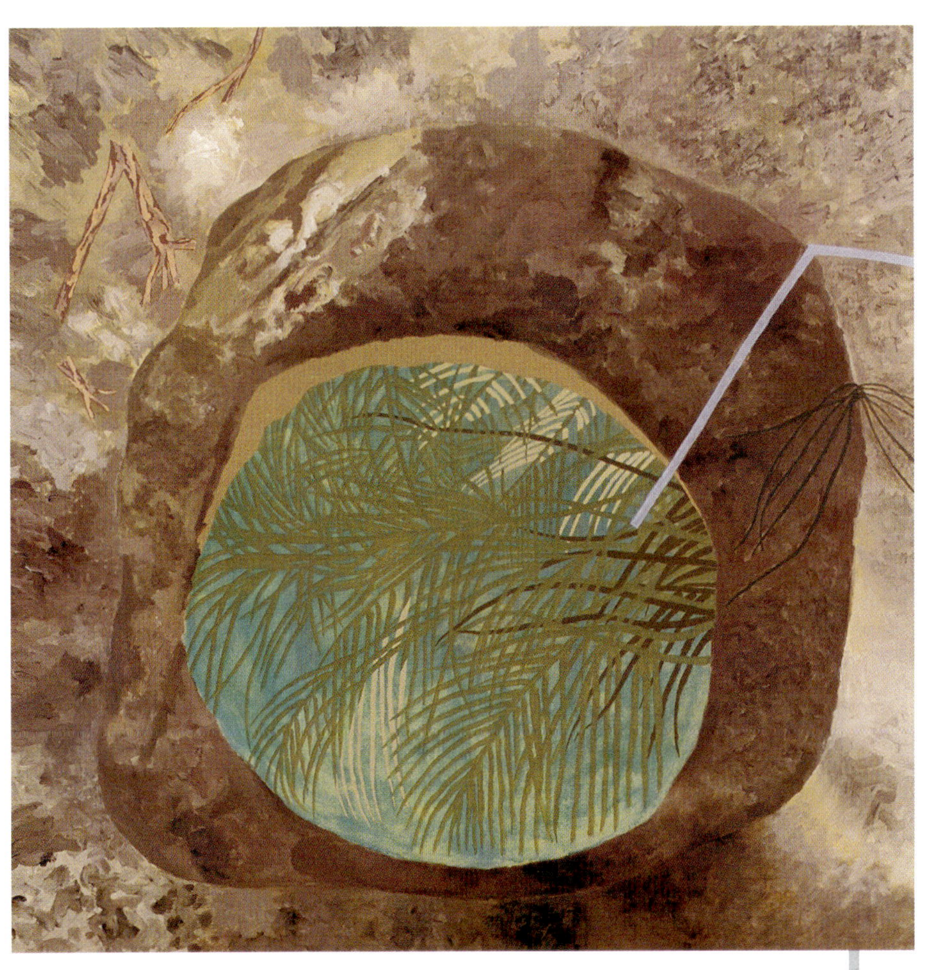

LOOKING INTO A WELL: FOLIAGE (2002)

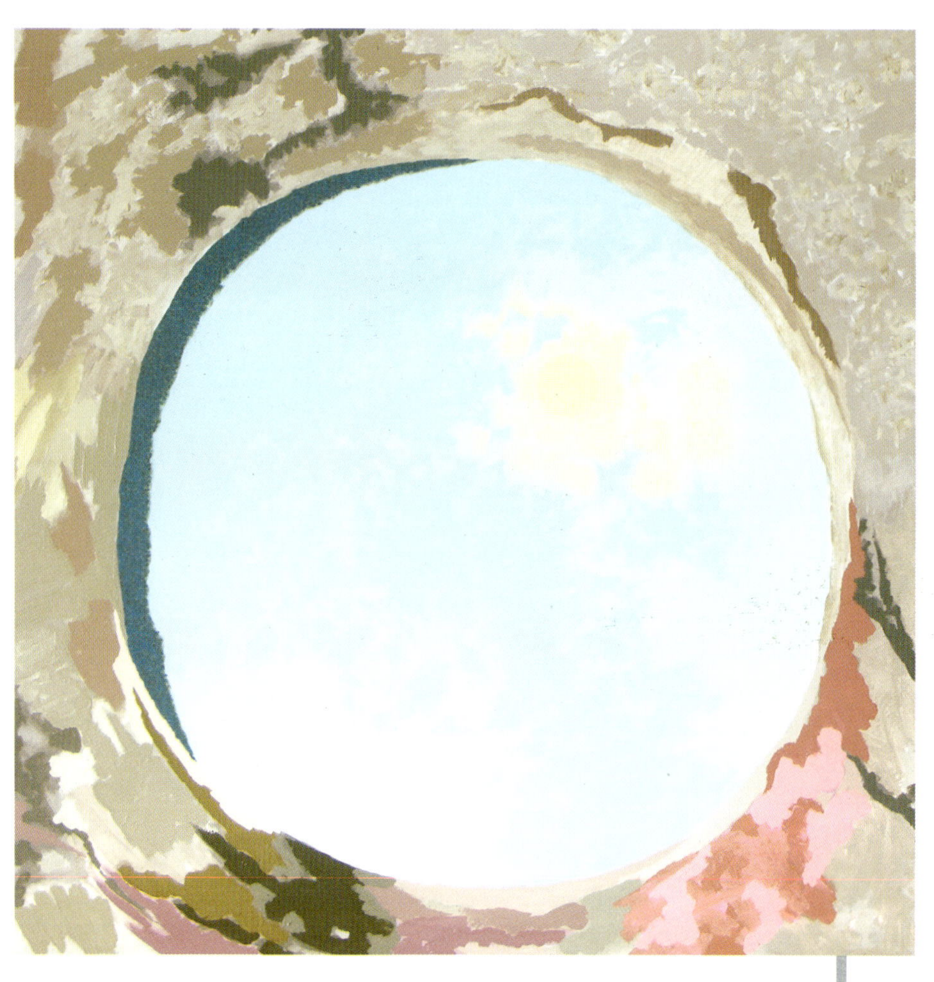

LOOKING INTO A WELL: THE SUN BEHIND CLOUDS (2003)

on moss and palm fronds, the roots striking up from the ground. In *Looking into a Well: The Sun Behind Clouds* (2003), which employs perhaps the most direct visual address of all the paintings in the *Wells* series, appearing to show exactly what it tells, we are offered a understated paradox: the solar glare, engauzed.

While the compressed or oblique narrative is one of Patel's primary inspirations, I would hazard the view that the crux of his work—whether in the properly figurative paintings or in those works that tend towards the abstractionist—is the attempted reconciliation of a sensuously apprehended particularity, treasured in itself, and an implied universal, standing beyond the incarnate particularity of forms. It is Patel's achievement to have attempted to effect this reconciliation, not through the quasi-philosophical devices that some artists, costumed as mystics, have deployed, but through the most tangible instruments of the painter's craft—through image, gesture, scene, and by way of the most practical problems of how to paint water, stone, sky and the figure of the survivor strained and distorted by crisis. Gieve Patel's paintings remind us that the most compelling artistic testimony comes from a consciousness that has combined artisanal devotion with visionary experience.

Bombay
Summer 2003

3.

The Startling View from the Studio

The Gemini syndrome is not the easiest of conditions, especially when two major artists have long been viewed as twins in terms of their pictorial interests and choices of treatment, their artistic socialization and viewing contexts. An external pressure could bear down on them, conflating their identities and blurring the difference between them; an internal pressure might force them to exchange a bonding weave for a separating edge. Fortunately, Gieve Patel and Sudhir Patwardhan have never permitted the perception that they are twinned artists to affect the course of their friendship, their collegiality, or the distinctive quests on which they have been engaged over the last several decades.

Patel (born 1940) and Patwardhan (born 1949) have taken the Western India megalopolis of Bombay for the locus of their activity; Patel lives in Colaba, its old colonial quarter, while Patwardhan lives in its sister city, Thane. Both artists have lived, either in their formative years or as young men, in other parts of India, so that their experience embraces other milieux than the strictly urban. And although Patel held his first solo exhibition in 1966, while Patwardhan held his 13 years later, both are prominent members of that generation of postcolonial Indian artists which articulated, over the late 1960s and early 1970s, a preoccupation with the specificities of a regional self shaped through engagement with its inherited histories and vibrant, immediate environment.

In their paintings, Patel, Patwardhan and their contemporaries addressed a range of subjects that had been banished from the high modernism of the preceding generation of Indian artists, whose sensibilities had been developed in relation to the Schools of Paris and New York. The emergent Indian avant-garde to which Patwardhan and Patel belonged looked elsewhere for sustenance, for experiences to memorialize and exemplars from whom to adapt idioms of attention: they scrutinized the everyday and the subaltern, the autobiographical and the fabular. It is important to remember, also, that they were not localist, but rather, internationalist in their attitude: they studied the strategies of the Mughal miniaturists, but also those of the Mexican muralists and the Sienese allegorists.

Within this formation of artists, Patel and Patwardhan have shared an ongoing conversation about formal problems and questions of representation. Through their concentration on certain kinds of urban figures, cast in the lineaments of a social class or existential predicament, they have traced the contours of a turbulent postcolonial modernity. Sensitive as they are to the figurative artist's ambivalent position as a voyeur-clairvoyant—one who watches other people's crises from the vantage point of his image-making practice—they have explored a productive tension between the solitude of the studio and the sociality of the public sphere.

At the same time, these artists shuttle between periods, styles and arrays of references to generate an intricate, substantial but rarely forbidding matrix against which the action of their paintings is played out. Strongly intercultural, they propose visions of the Now that are shot through with vivid elements taken from Giotto or the Safahvi masters, Piero della Francesca or Masaccio: the afterlife of these predecessors animates their present in sophisticated, unpredictable ways, indicating the persistence of instinct through the centuries or the manifestation of a psychological tendency across cultural boundaries.

Both painters have attempted, throughout their careers, to keep faith with the enigma of expressiveness while representing people bound together by situations, without lapsing into the dryly programmatic tenor that sometimes afflicts figurative painters who locate their protagonists within a definite social scenario. If Patel has sought fresh purchase on realism by attending to such problems of pictorial fiction as how to paint a stretch of grass, the skin of unruffled water, exposed brick or a verge of moss in their dense palpability, Patwardhan has evolved a heroic anatomy of torsion, focusing on such details of the labouring body as the gripping fist, the amplified shoulders, the tense wrist or a sinewy arm expanded by incessant effort.

II.

Patwardhan has often emphasized the quality of attentiveness by which the artist can grasp his subject: not by framing it in a single moment of epiphany, but through a constant shuttling between proximate and distant viewpoints that yields an intermediate, shifting yet visionary sense of reality. Patel, for his part, has treated the body as the bearer of an intimate knowledge of constraint and transcendence: if it is vulnerable to stray or systematic acts of violence in his account, it is also capable of shouldering the freight of historical significance. Both artists have been captivated by the possibility of revealing what is secret: they reflect on the idioms of living that the city allows the individual or the group, whether at the obvious level of street or neighbourhood or, more allusively and tantalizingly, when approached through half-curtained windows or doors left ajar.

Working as they do in a tradition that approaches the figural and transcendent through the objects of the tangible world, both artists have been fascinated by the varying temperaments and temperatures of the body. Their paintings bear testimony to the publicly demonstrated body of the worker, demonstrator, trucker, beggar or madman in the street; but also to the private body with its capacity for surprise and elusiveness. Looking beneath the normalities of the named skin, they pierce the innocuous exterior of an accepted gender identity or established social role. Between them, Patwardhan and Patel affirm the possibility that figurative painting retains the power to ask important questions of the self and the world.

Patel may depict on an armless beggar being fed by a girl, or a scribe writing a letter to a construction worker's dictation; Patwardhan may translate an accident in a train station into an elegiac tableau or impart regal grandeur to a man sitting on a bentwood chair in a cafe. Patel has often waded out into the life of the street to produce, in his paintings, makeshift spaces of belonging in which individuals encounter one another, or communicate with one another, in mysterious, non-discursive ways: the action of these dramas, in which public space is rendered momentarily private, cannot easily be deciphered. Patwardhan has been equally active in his interpretation of crucial moments of collective action. He has been preoccupied with organizing his figures into groups, whether random crowds, orderly mobilizations or mobs, maintaining the density of detail in such a way as to pick out individuals while portraying the swarming energy of a multitude.

These memorable images remind us that both Patel and Patwardhan have been, to varying degrees, observers and participants in the situations they address. They are, to invoke a description that I developed in my 2004 study of Patwardhan's art, complicit observers. Neither painter stands aloof from his society or its driving currents; even when an image appears detached and clinical, look closely and you will see that an empathetic or critical investment of emotion binds the representing consciousness to the subject being represented. The trope of complicity is, to me, a vital one: it underlines the relationship of observer to subject in an intensely political manner; it dismantles the myth of the neutral observer and the folklore of the impassioned participant, obliging us to question both objectivity and behalfism.

The complicit observer, as I have described this position, partakes in the unfolding destinies of his subjects, his empathy explicit in his painterly treatment. I find the sinister undertone in the adjective 'complicit' most apposite: to me, it foregrounds those nuances of guilt at representation and voyeuristic furtiveness of observation, that acknowledgement of the shared onus of existence and the push-pull between belonging and remoteness, which characterize all honest figurative art. The complicit observer, as I have argued before, establishes his own vulnerability as a subjectivity engaged in the lifeworld it depicts, and so initiates a possibility of community with his subjects.

Vigorously informed as their work is by an awareness of the asymmetries of opportunity and attainment that divide Indian society, neither Patel nor Patwardhan ever becomes didactic or hortatory. Within the larger sweep of public events, their figures act out private dramas of grief, anxiety, uncertainty and resilience: Patwardhan draws his protagonists largely from among the urban proletariat or the tenuously perched middle class; Patel, from among the city's marginal, deviant or eccentric floating population. Despite the fact that this subaltern figure is the unit of measurement for social anguish or private unease, it is never a victim; on the contrary, it is almost always a survivor.

III.

In the recent works that form their New York exhibition, the meaning-making self is the subject of Patwardhan and Patel's scrutiny. This is especially true of Patwardhan's recent suite of paintings, in which he confronts the remembering and desiring self as it composes a private world from circumstance and dream, imagining an ethos into being rather than simply accepting the world as it is. Patwardhan has periodically revisited the theme of the artist in his studio, the expressive self at the observation post from which it conducts its surveillance of experience. But the tenor of autobiography rings more clearly in these paintings than ever before in his art: he probes, subtly, the deep contexts of family, artistic practice and lineages of image-making. A man stares at a canvas; the reflection of the buildings outside are recast, in the glass front of his cabinet, into a Diebenkorn abstractionist landscape. Another man looks out of the window of his studio at a vista that is strongly reminiscent of the landscape in a Giotto painting.

Indeed, Patwardhan's figures are frequently liminal: they stand at a threshold, either spatially, or at the edge of a decision. He is fascinated by the advent of the figure in pictorial space: how someone enters a room, dominates a moment, alters a colloquial, everyday gesture into a ceremonial act. In these new paintings, a young woman walks into a room looking anxious, an older woman buys a railway ticket, a cyclist passes a lake on an overcast day presaging flood. Such settings, ordinary and suburban in themselves, are transmuted by a palette that might suggest Raphael or Balthus; the artist resets the relationships between figure and context, detail and whole, so that the play of scale enhances and magnifies the workaday into the near-epic. He operates through synecdoche: a hand holds the key to an individual's character, an edge of skin symbolizes the encounter between person and environment, self and other. In these recent works, too, he dwells with renewed sensuous regard on folds, crimps, ripples in fabric, flesh or hillsides: symptoms of the erotic.

Patel's recent works turn on the pivotal mysteries of creation and destruction. His concern is with the cycle of activities—intimate, artisanal, everyday—that make up the business of life: the verb gestures of putting an object together, gazing at others involved in their routines, repairing a slipper; and, in the animal world, of eating an animal that chance has delivered into your hands. Even when they seem passive, static or withdrawn, Patel's figures—human or bird—are intensely alive and committed to an activity, however inward and private it may be. It strikes me that, while Patwardhan's paintings are often about collectives in motion, in conversation, in dispute and conflict, Patel's paintings often feature groups that are the interwoven sum of unspoken privacies.

In a recent work that renders homage to the building of a ship in one of Bombay's fisher-colonies, the figures come together limb by limb; as it were, component by component. An arm, concealed by the drape of a magenta sari, like the scaled-down wing of a Greek Nike, meets the eye; then a dog, its brown skin-folds gaining definition in an air made pungent by drying fish; and finally the eye comes to rest on the blaze of sun above water, one arm of the city suspended above the bay like a mirage. The content of Patel's compressed narratives remains unspelt-out, withheld as in the paintings of Piero della Francesca, whom Patel admires. Consider, for instance, Patel's painting *Madman in the Street* (2005), in which the figure stares fixedly at us, garlanded like a sacrificial victim; our attention is seized, however, by the masked figure behind him, a figure seemingly theatrical in inspiration, whose fixed, ceremonial smile we cannot adequately decode.

For a figurative artist, Patel exhibits a high degree of abstraction: his paintings are rich in plasmic sheets of sky, flame, sea, well water and reflections in well water. His preferred texture, a quirky, mottled tapestry, signifies a myriad teemingness redolent of microscopic life while also suggesting a fluid connection among all beings and things. And indeed, an auratic, transfigurative impulse has increasingly come to charge the paintings both of Patel and Patwardhan since the early 1990s. Each artist has placed, in recent years, a wager on transcendence.

Patel has worked on a series of wells, the water serving as an interface between worlds, a mystery of passage, a site for the recovery of the self's lost contents. Patwardhan has meditated on the panoramic view of an industrial township, situating it in the context of the cosmic cycles of time: the transient architectures of the moment are contained by the revolving seasons, and the boisterous journey of the secular self through life is translated into a stately pilgrimage. In each case, the artist steps outside the space of the singular self and reminds us that resources of regeneration await our attention in the larger domain of being that lies beyond the ego. The view from the studio is not merely a sedate surveyor's menu of imagined landscapes; it is a startling reminder that the aesthetic is a mode by which the consciousness can be tricked, ambushed or persuaded into expanding, sometimes radically, beyond its customary or long-guarded spectrum of responses.

Bombay

September 2005–January 2006

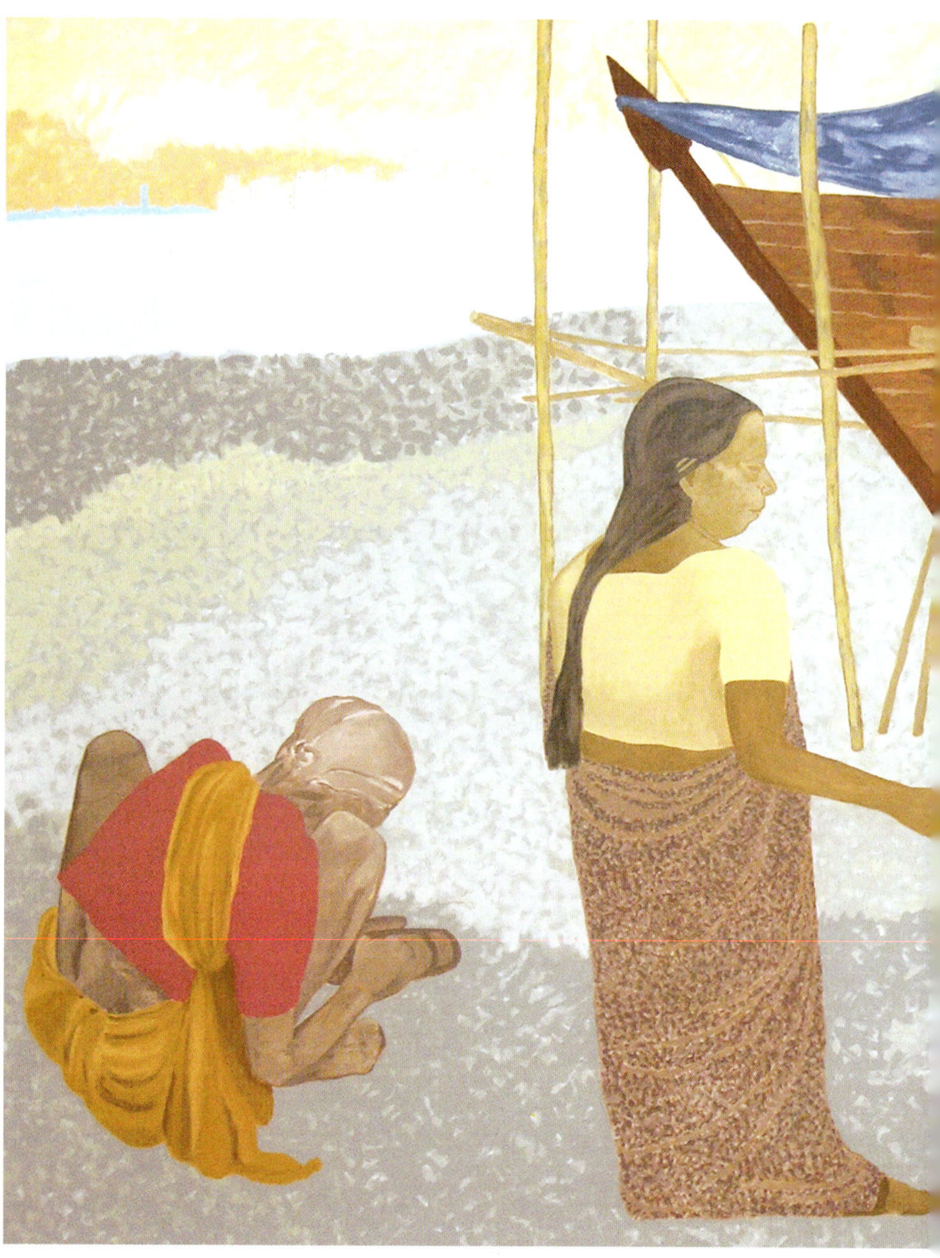

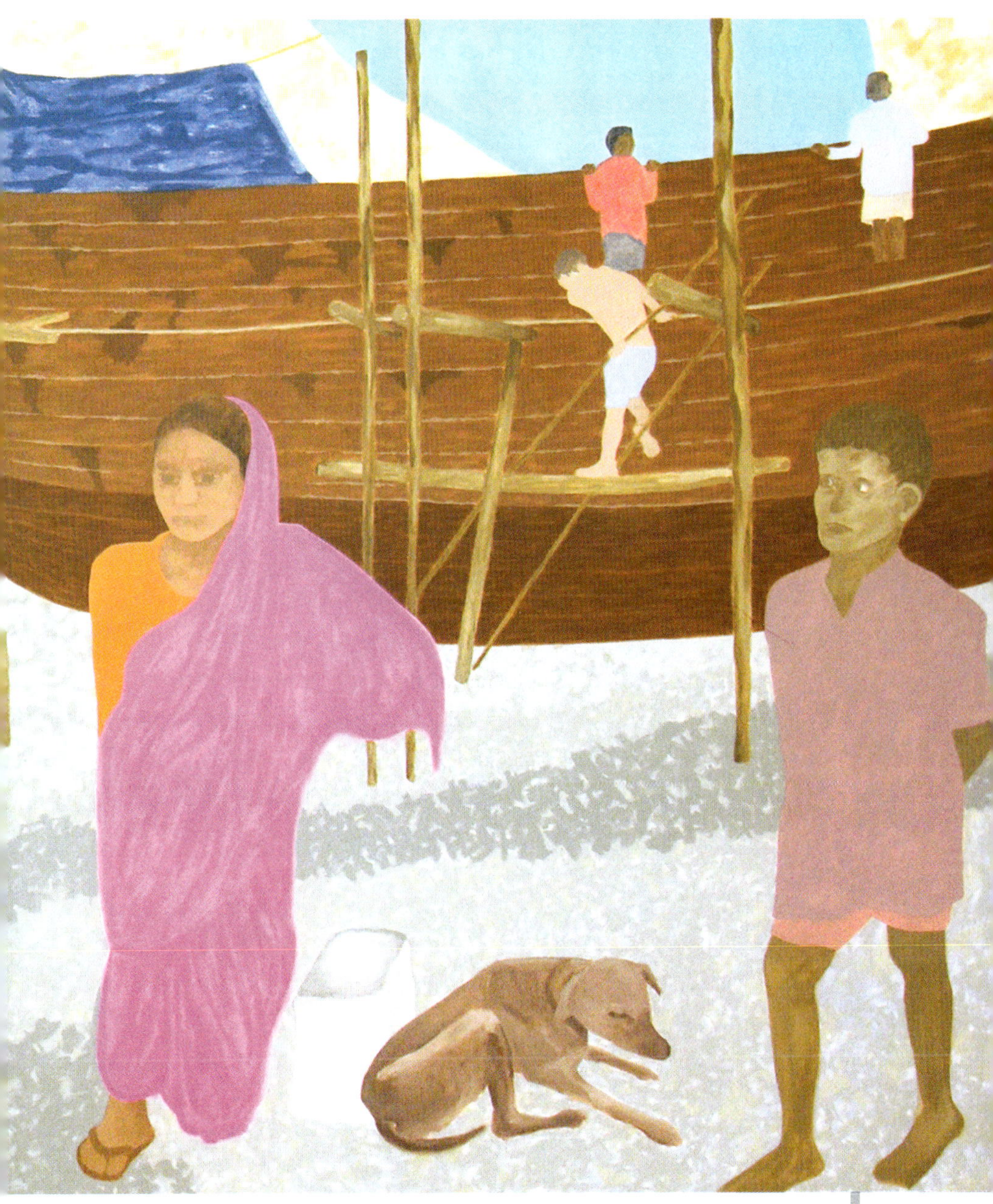

SHIP BUILDING IN MUMBAI (2005)

4.

To Break and To Branch

Gieve Patel's sculptures register a departure for this distinguished painter, poet and playwright. These elaborations in terracotta, bronze and fibreglass are not marked by the hesitancy of the beginner; they possess an instinctive assurance, the images crisply conceived, the execution measured, the unfolding thought embodied precisely in the evolving grammar of the objects. And then it strikes us. Formally, these images—the pointing hand with the broken thumb or rhizomatic, tubercular fingers; the stroke-battered head, dignified even in mortal injury; the body streaming into the landscape—are the key gestures of his paintings, abstracted and isolated, heightened beyond narrative detail to be radiantly themselves. As emotional provocations, Patel's sculptures draw together the themes of desire and woundedness, lust and betrayal, which have exercised his poetry and drama for four decades.

Two figures from myth dominate this suite of works, one culled from Graeco-Roman mythology, the other recruited from the Indian epics: Daphne and Eklavya. Daphne, water nymph and daughter of a river god, becomes the object of Apollo's affections; but the sun god's love

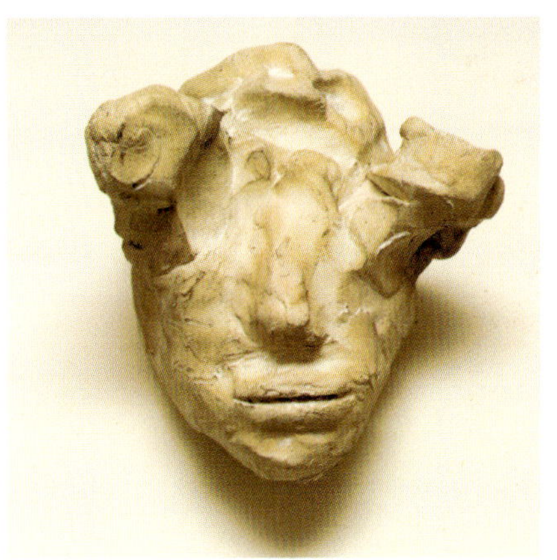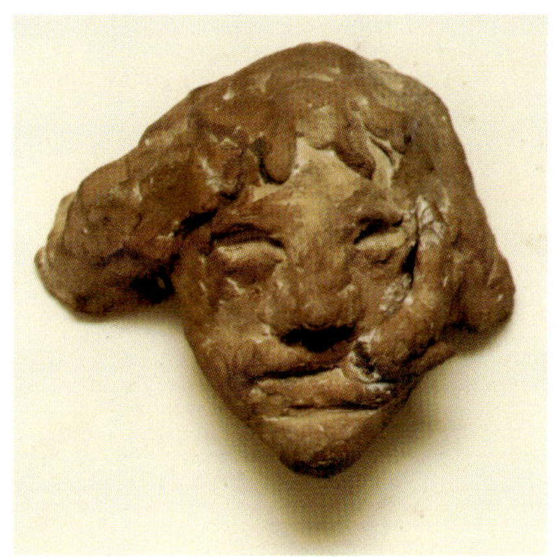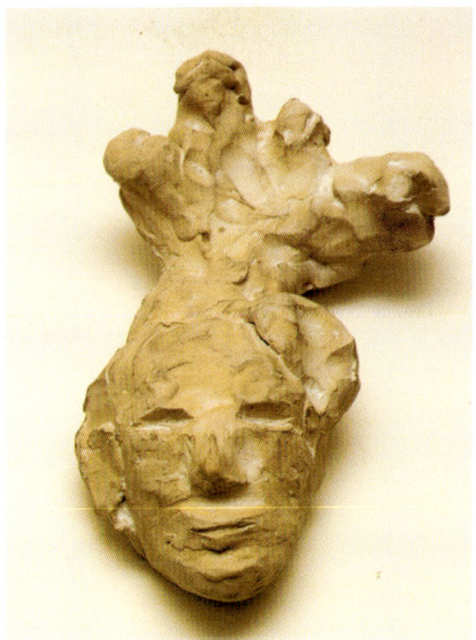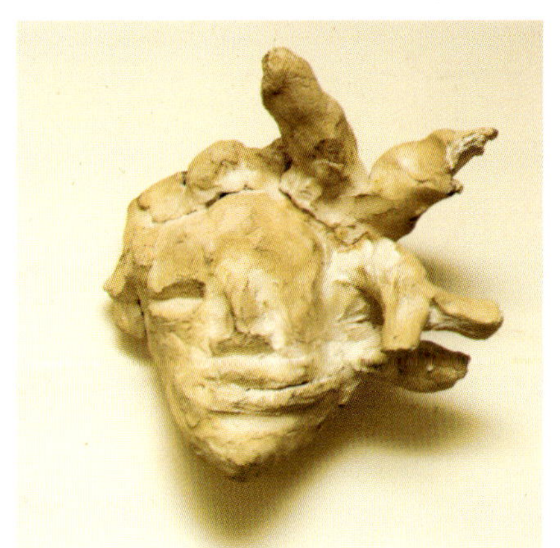

FROM THE 'DAPHNE' SERIES (2006)

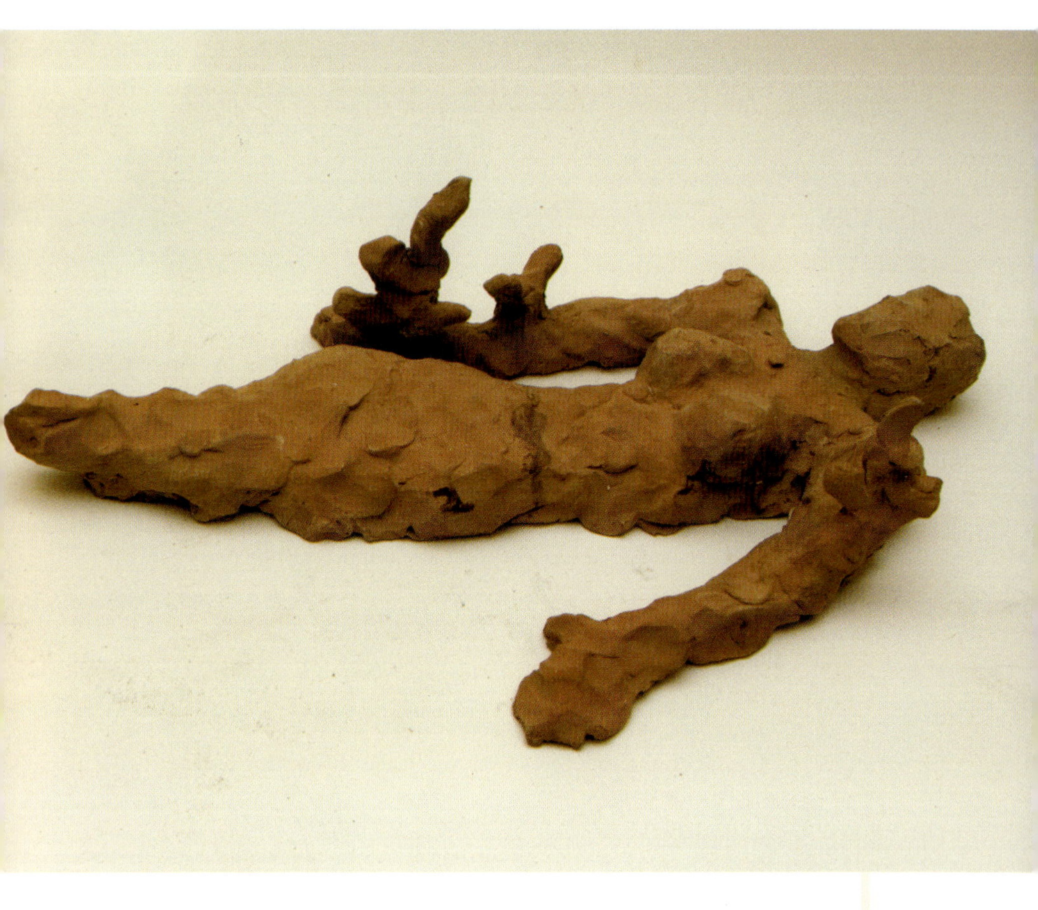

FROM THE 'DAPHNE' SERIES (2006)

manifests itself as unruly lust, and he chases her to the river bank, the harmony of his music and prosody forgotten. Unwilling to become a victim so readily, Daphne prays for redemption: she is saved from rape by being turned into a laurel, and her divine pursuer's fingers close on the leaves that spring from her flesh. Soon, she is a shrub, and he is left inconsolable at his haste and folly. The story, originally an episode in the cycles of Aegean folklore, is movingly told by Ovid in his classic *Metamorphoses*, was captured memorably in marble, centuries later, by Bernini, and has inspired countless lyrical, narrative and pictorial interpretations as a topos of love running amok and causing its own defeat, desire transmogrified into wanton destructiveness.

Eklavya, prince of hunters, cannot hope to approach Drona, the magisterial warrior-priest who is guru to the princes of Hastinapura. His veneration bridges social distance imaginatively, and he sculpts a clay statue of the preceptor in the forest, practicing archery before it, honing his skills. His solitude is broken when, one day, the Hastinapura princes enter the forest. In a spontaneous display of prowess, Eklavya defeats Arjuna, their generation's leading archer; Arjuna demands to know who has taught him and is amazed to hear his own guru named. Angry, he demands that Drona rectify the situation; Drona confronts Eklavya in the forest and asks, as his guru-dakshina or tutorial fee, for the hunter-prince's thumb, destroying his future as an archer for ever. This story from the Mahabharata has, ever after, served as a template for the oppression of the weaker by the more powerfully entrenched castes.

Both Daphne and Eklavya are figures maimed or ruined by forces that demanded their submission: the nymph who defies the sun god's lust, the hunter who dares to equal the warrior-prince, both punished for their transgression. Patel interprets both figures, and other presences from myth, dream and waking life, with the energy of an artist responding

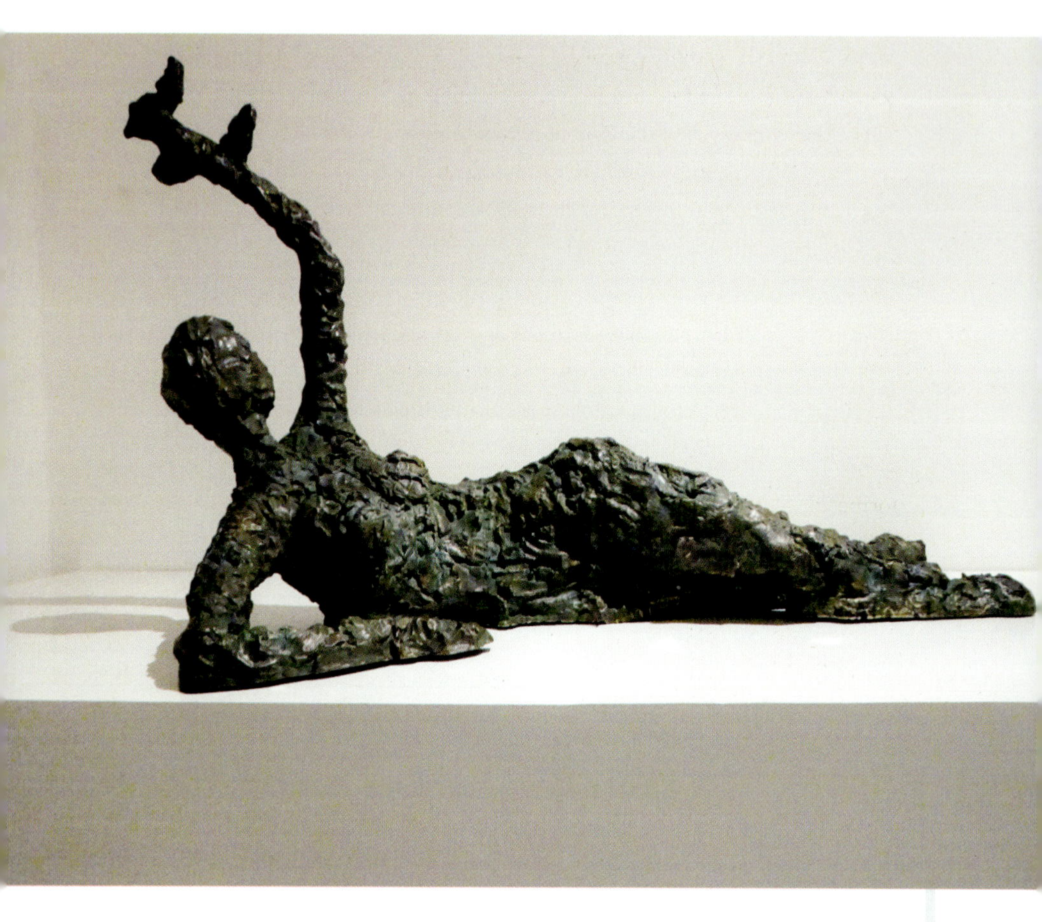

FROM THE 'DAPHNE' SERIES (2006)

vigorously to the promptings of his material. The impress of the shaping hand is everywhere in these works: in the textures of flow and knot; in heads that turn sharply on their shoulders; in the twisting of a wrist and the torsion of a female body that is vulnerable as a girl and resilient as the earth; in mouths that open to allow water and weeds to gush out, images that mark a persistence of concern from Patel's paintings, being strongly reminiscent of such paintings of Patel's from the 1980s as *Crushed Head* and *Drowned Woman*. Breaking and branching are the crucial movements that captivate his attention: nodes of pain, but also of growth.

Daphne and Eklavya have the fulcrum of pain in common: we come upon them at occasions of intense suffering, understanding and transformation. We gaze upon Daphne, just as her fingers break into leaves; we discover Eklavya with the cut thumb dangling from his palm by a thread of skin.

Daphne is a creature of violent, forced transition; she is held, always, at the threshold of transformation. In Ovid's *Metamorphoses*, she is a victim of the transgressive behaviour of the god Apollo, who is not only Reason and Art personified, but is also in love with her; strangely, he expresses his love as a brutal desire for conquest. The Daphne myth has fascinated Patel for many years; in his poem, 'Squirrels in Washington DC', he describes her predicament as a 'freedom in transit / between cage and cage'. Eklavya is a nishada boy who aspires to kshatriya skills: the perennial outsider who challenges the status quo, and is punished for his transgression. Patel has been preoccupied with the tribal presence, technically excluded but in actuality integral, in mainstream Indian life; his play, *Mister Behram*, revolves around the crisis of a tribal boy adopted by a Parsi lawyer and brought up as his son. Formally, Patel's Eklavya figure bears a strong affinity to Giacometti's axiate and attenuated figure.

*

Although Daphne and Eklavya are central to Patel's suite of sculptures, figures such as the many-breasted woman and the giant human-arboreal mask act as vital presences as well. The woman with many breasts symbolizes vegetative proliferation, an image of abundance that provokes, at the same time, an unease at rampant hypertrophy. The giant mask, seemingly frontal, is meant to be seen in the round; it communicates itself as a metaphor for growth, the mask concealing the energies of a powerful tree draped in creepers. The woman as sphinx also occurs here, reminiscent of Sufiya Zenobia in Rushdie's *Shame*, a terror swaddled in mystery; she reappears as a hortus, a body turned into a garden. Patel makes reference to the classical nude, but models it through a deliberately rough and ready notation. The female nude is a body in torsion here: a Z-shaped line of energy travelling from the upraised arm to the arm resting on the ground, the woman twisting on her own axis, turning into a tree even as she looks on, unable to stop the process.

Patel's is a sophisticated eye: like many visual artists, critics and curators, he carries a visual archive in memory; he makes connections through cited gestures, quotations of a hand or a head, a twist of the body or a turn of the wrist. These could be viewed as studies in the persistence of forms—*das Nachleben der Antike*, the afterlife of the classical, in a phrase beloved of Aby Warburg—especially since some of these forms resonate with Velázquez's *Rokeby Venus* or a Rubens mermaid, a detail that Patel picked from the Northern Baroque master's pictorial epithalamion, a cycle of paintings celebrating the marriage of Catherine de' Medici to the French Dauphin.

Patel's trove of sculptures represents work done at white heat during a two-week residency at Studio Sukriti, Jaipur, a sculptors' and ceramicists' collective. The artist delights, especially, in the passage of the image from one medium to another, as from terracotta to bronze, or terracotta

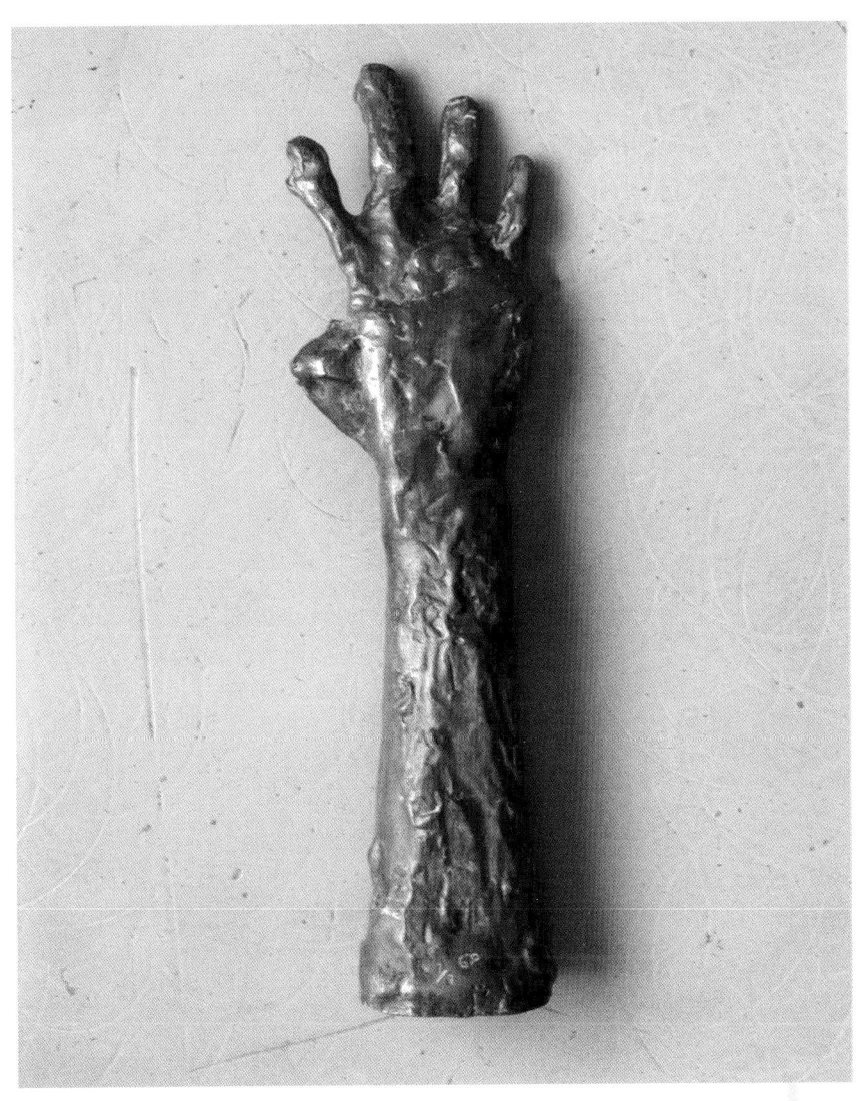

FROM THE 'EKLAVYA' SERIES (2006)

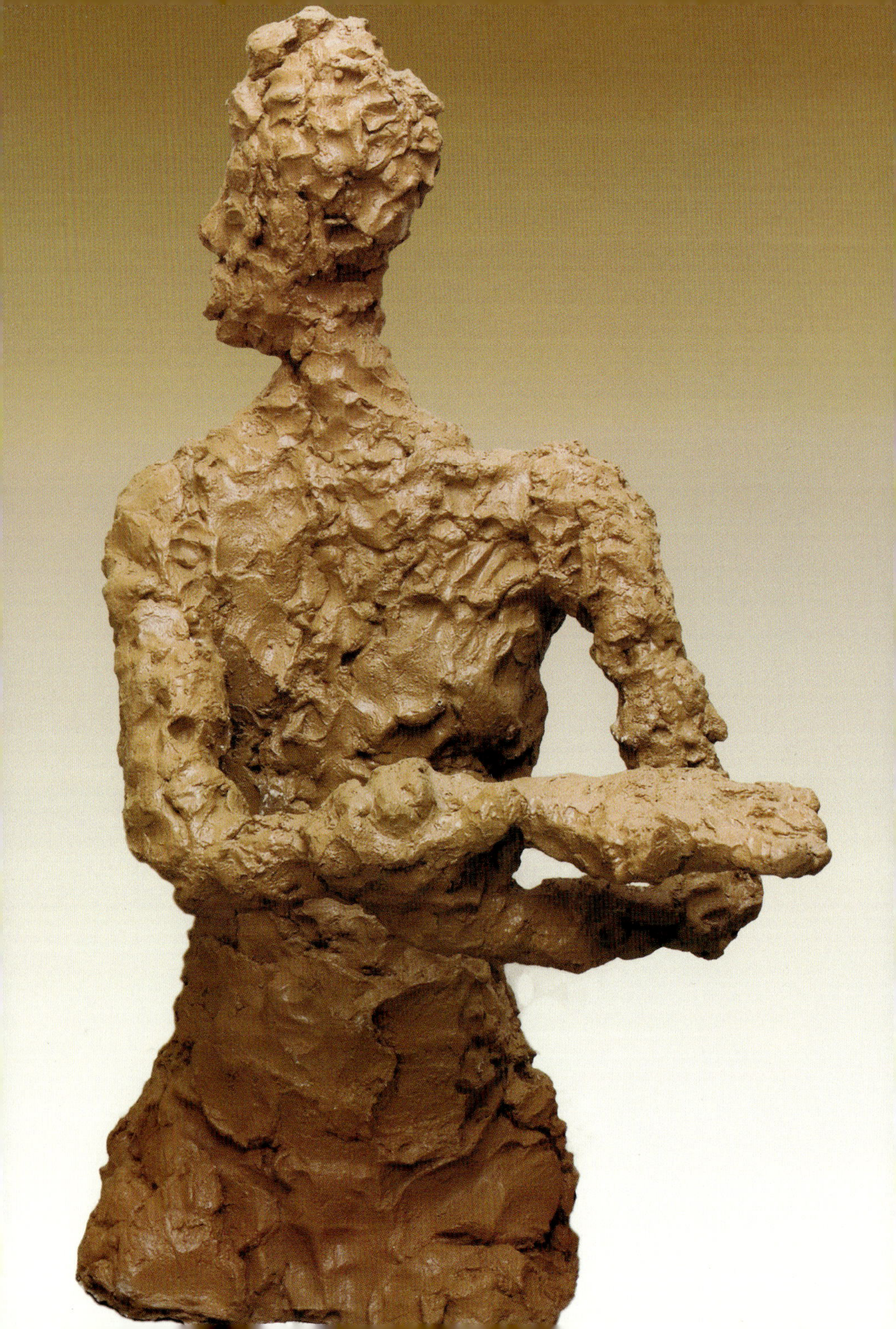

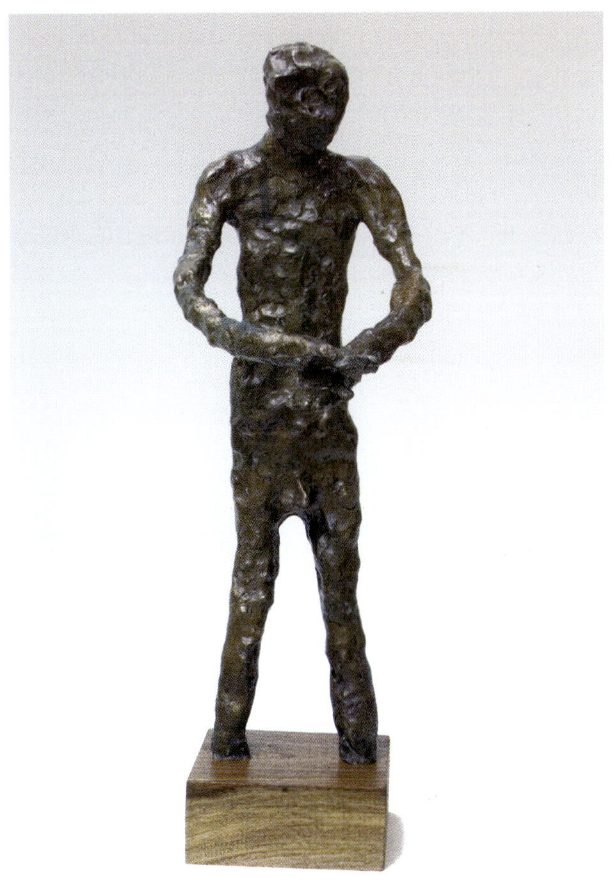

FROM THE 'EKLAVYA' SERIES (2006)

to fibreglass; in this sense, the present exhibition is linked together by acts of translation.

Mud has always been important to Patel; it takes him back to his Nargol childhood; it appears often in his poems and paintings. Now, it manifests itself as the clay in which his sculptures are originally brought to life; this is the first time he has worked in this medium. Not coincidentally, I have been fascinated by the mobility of the hand that recurs as a motif in his paintings, and now in his sculptures: Patel's is a haptic consciousness, the grip and grasp not merely holding but also shaping the world's material into an image. He corroborates this view, taking delight in the gestural nature of the new work: 'I've used a lump of clay as an ear, a gash as a mouth. The clay has the capacity to speak, I just have to nudge it.'

For the four monumental sculptures, Patel used assistants from the Sukriti Studio. This is the first time Patel has worked with assistants, and in a space outside his studio, apart from occasional print-making ventures in the past. And, certainly, this is the first time he has ceded so much of the image-making process to other hands and to happenstance. Sculpture, we are reminded, is an art dependent on climatic and edaphic variables that are often beyond the sculptor's control, or must be skilfully modulated: these include the behaviour of material under the shaping influence of stress, friability, temperature, ambient moisture or lack of it, calcium content in the water used to shape the clay, and so forth. Patel admits to having been assailed by anxieties during and after his periods of work in Jaipur, but also records his pleasure at the emergence of unexpected results. He vividly recalls the day when students and workmen at the studio, under his supervision, flung clay at the largest of his wire armatures, bringing to life a recumbent figure with her arm thrown out in a gesture that might be despair, self-protection or, very simply, a sudden bursting forth into leaf.

The artist has translated this formative gesture of clay-flinging into a painterly strategy, in creating the solitary, large-scale watercolour drawing that accompanies the sculptures. In this work on paper, significantly enough, the clay-flinging takes on the character of stoning, so that this new figure is neither Eklavya nor Daphne, but, to my mind, a third: Stephen, the first martyr, garlanded and pelted with pebbles by the irate mob that accuses him of blasphemy. The truth-speaker, slain by those who cannot bear the illumination of truth, is a worthy successor to the nymph turned tree and the wounded archer, and perhaps points towards a direction that Gieve Patel may be ready to take as he continues his exploration of the twinned processes of breaking and branching, suffering and insight.

Bombay/Jaipur
September 2006—May 2007

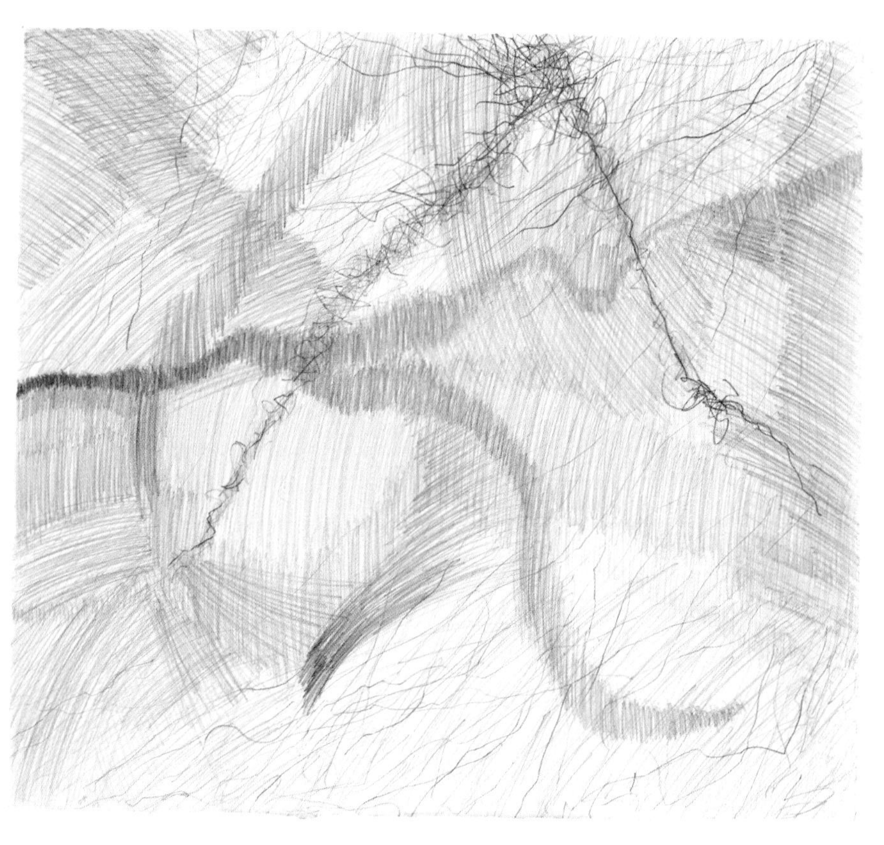

CLOUD, 13 (2007)

5.

Sight as Covenant

GIEVE PATEL: WELLS, CLOUDS, SKULLS

I. Transiting among Three Domains

Gieve Patel has always looked the world unflinchingly in the eye, recording its challenges to the bodied self in all their horror and rawness. And while the pictorial accounts emerging from this confrontation with the real have been terse and unsentimental, Patel has always rendered the human subject in the wounded splendour of its resilience. Unlikely candidates for heroism at first sight, Patel's marginal and eccentric figures play their role in dramas that are set, for the most part, in the public and unstable space of the street. Over a career that now spans 45 years, Patel has invited us to share in such powerful and memorable images as that of a crushed head, an old man carrying bananas home through the rain, a madman navigating the street, a drowned woman, an armless beggar being fed by a girl, an illiterate labourer dictating a letter to a scribe, a body left to carrion birds on a beach, a child rescued from a fire. His paintings have borne testimony to the unpredictability of everyday life in a postcolonial society, as represented by its principal metropolis,

Bombay, and also by loci in its rural hinterland; these images speak to us of the sweep of historical change as well as the micro-politics of intimate violence.

On the other hand, with increasing frequency since the early 1990s, Patel has also reached out to the transcendental dimension of experience, with such vivid images as the man clutching at a peacock as if it were his soul leaping out of his body, the white bird soaring above a sun-drenched village pond and its wallowing buffaloes, and his continuing series of paintings of wells dug like probes into the obstinacy of rural earth.

And indeed, if the paintings and drawings gathered together to form Patel's exhibition, *Wells Clouds Skulls*, are any indication, there seems to have been a remarkable letting-up of the nervous tension that has so far characterized this artist's relationship with his subject matter. These works offer us abundant evidence of a new lightness of spirit, an amplitude of engagement, a willingness to embrace rather than interrogate the world.

These paintings and drawings spring from three specific visual experiences: those of looking into a well; looking at clouds coursing through the sky; and looking at an anatomical exhibit that allows one to gauge, even if by means of simulation, what lies beneath one's own skin. These occasions go far beyond the usual sharpness of a moment of observation, of the kind that anyone attuned to the visual arts would be used to. These are not acts merely of observation; rather, they are epiphanic covenants with some system or narrative larger than the individual self. They are signs that guarantee, in some impalpable but ringingly definite way, the individual's belonging in some vaster scheme or momentum. To phrase it in the language of Indic philosophy, Patel appears to transit among three lokas, three domains of being, in this constellation of paintings and drawings: the netherworld; the heavens; and the human, earthly, mortal condition.

These works recall to mind the story of the god Vishnu, in his avatar as the Brahmin dwarf Vamana, in the Bhagavat Purana: in order to humble the demon emperor Bali, Vamana asks him for as much territory as he can cover in three paces; upon this wish being granted, the dwarf magnifies himself to cosmic proportions, covers the earth in one stride, the heavens in the second, and asks Bali what remains. At which the emperor, his ego broken, offers the god his own head. With a single gesture, he recognizes the inevitable dissolution of all glory and ascendancy; is pushed bodily into the netherworld; and passes, his spirit purified, into the paradise of the elect. In his moment of transformative insight, Bali becomes no more and no less than the awakened consciousness, incarnating the contest between the freight of wilfulness and the potential for redemption; his body, with all its appetites and desires, falls away.

In *Wells Clouds Skulls*, we feel—more strongly than ever before in Patel's art—the urgent presence of a consciousness meditating on the processes of resolution and dissolution, substantiality and evanescence. And significantly, the human figure, which has been Patel's chosen vehicle of articulation for nearly five decades, is notably absent in these paintings and drawings.

II. The Well as an Occasion of Vision

Patel was first drawn to wells during childhood vacations spent on the ancestral estate in south Gujarat, north of Bombay. He recalls the simple but compelling mystery of the well, its surface changing with the season, low and flat in summer, brimming in the monsoon. It was not until 1991, though—after he had turned 50—that the artist thought of addressing this experience in his work. This has led to an ongoing sequence of wells produced over a two-decade period: wells recorded or imagined at various times of day and night, different seasons and elevations, their

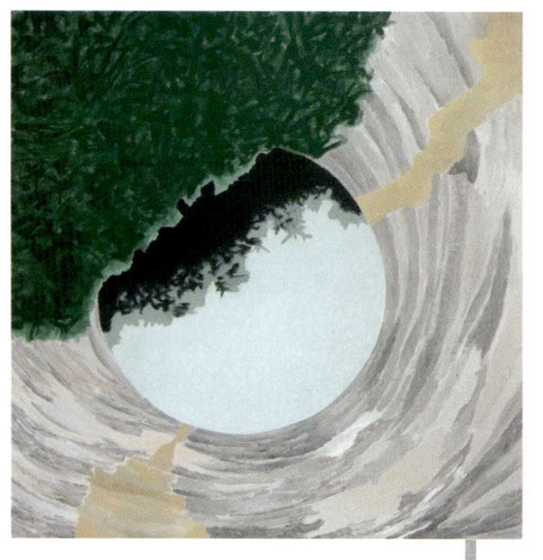

LOOKING INTO A WELL: THE GREEN BUSH
(2008)

LOOKING INTO A WELL: BOUGAINVILLEA
(2010)

surface holding a diversity of elements and yet, instructively—as Patel's friend and fellow painter, Sudhir Patwardhan, has remarked[1]—never the face of the man looking in. If Patel probes the earth and what lies beneath—the springs of life, the foundations of drought—he also explores the need of a Narcissus alert to his weakness and committed to overcoming his fascination with himself in favour of a wider curiosity about the world as it reveals itself through images. As Patwardhan observes: 'It is the act of looking itself that is being portrayed here and not the subject. Could the image of the well be an image of the eye?'[2] Patel's wells can indeed resemble a lens; usually, though, the surfaces of his wells suggest Petri dishes tapestried with bacterial cultures, the residues of stratified archaeological digs, or archives of weeds and mirrored palms, repositories of fallen leaves, trailing creepers and troves of flowers. Since Patel does not insist on the push/pull conventions of realistic representation, the well can sometimes act as an unidentified object, landing among the sienna and ochre of a field. The three paintings of wells that Patel presents here, executed over 2008–2010, are the largest he has essayed: each is 8 ft x 8 ft, the scale a metaphor for the cosmos.

In *Looking into a Well: The Green Bush* (2008), Patel disorients us with a stone whirlpool, a vortex quarried from flinty strata, deposits of chalk, looking into which (or rather, at which) we are seized by an attack of vertigo. The world seems upside down, and the composition appears to have benefited from the conflation of several viewer positions. This particular vision of a well suggests a broken eyeball of water, which holds sky and vegetation; the season is clearly the monsoon, for an abundant burst of rich green animates the painting, leaving room for a luminous edge where the vegetation meets its reflected double.

Looking into a Well: Bougainvillaea (2010) is a study in greens and browns, dominated by bare branches, dry walls and a curiously flat

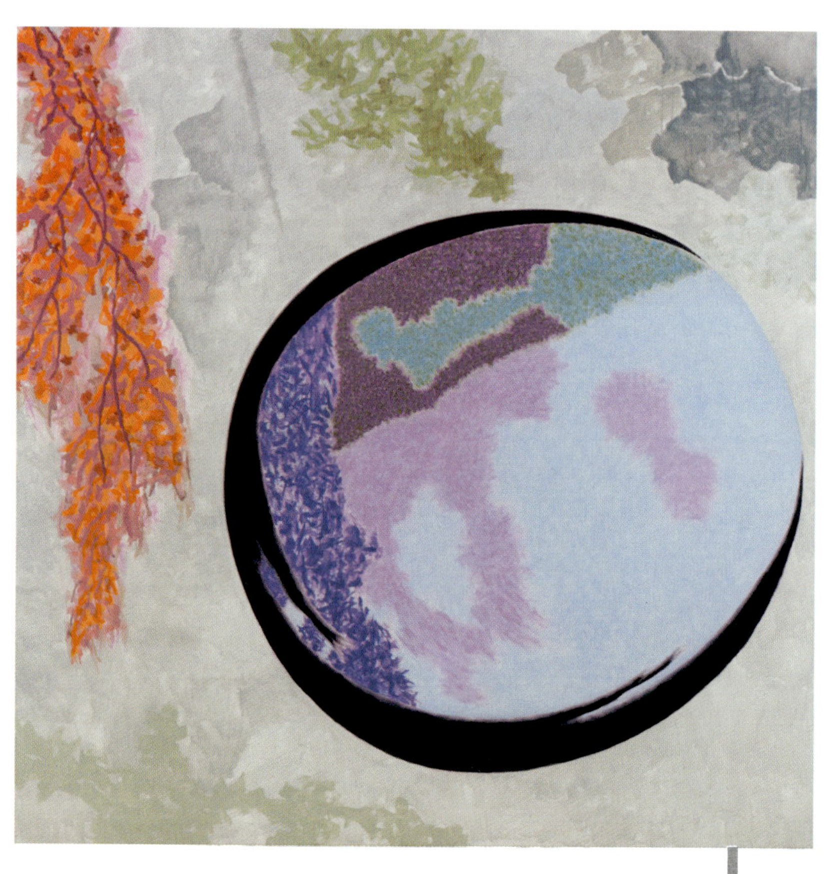

LOOKING INTO A WELL: A SPRAY OF BLOSSOMS
(2010)

bottom of water. At first sight, it resembles a deep blank eye; looked at with greater attention, it opens to unveil interior distances, mapped detail by detail. We may detect, here, the incipient sapling and the dry root, the prompting of leaf, the thrum of life. The well seems to brace itself for an autumn in Gujarat, that brief truce between the elements that marks the end of the monsoon and the onset of winter in peninsular India.

Looking into a Well: A Spray of Blossoms (2010) is a painting for spring. A jubilation in festive violets and oranges, set off by celadon and mulberry, it is aggregated from the play of granularity and dissolution, delivered in sweeping brush-strokes. The events on the unruffled surface of the water imply the stone of a hill, the passage of a cloud, and a spray of flowers caught up in the momentum of the rushing wind. Paradoxically enough, here, to look down is to look up; and indeed, to look into a depth is to risk falling or being disoriented, losing oneself. It is a moment fraught with the potentiality of self-dissolution.

III. An Atlas of Clouds

The observation of the movement of clouds is one of the oldest visualization and divinatory devices known to humankind: if children play this game as a diversion, some Vajrayana Buddhist monks treat it as a predictive exercise and Leonardo da Vinci used it as the basis of an exercise for the imagination. Patel made his very first cloud drawing in the 1980s, and then, after a long gap, worked on occasional cloud drawings through the 1990s. In his drawings of clouds shown in the present exhibition, rendered between 2002 and 2009, he explores the real and imagined geographies of the upper air: forms that knot together, coalesce, drift apart. He delights in the sheer diversity of linear form,

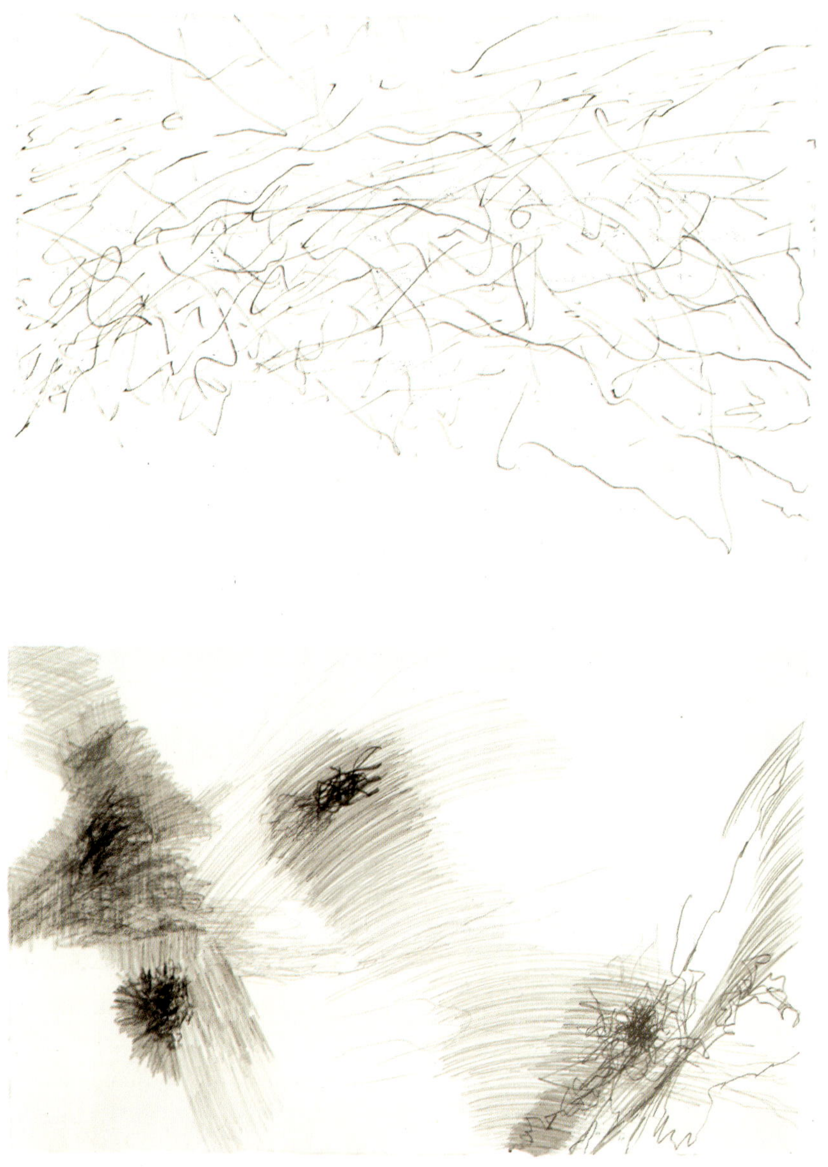

CLOUD, 3 (2009) and CLOUD, 14 (2007)

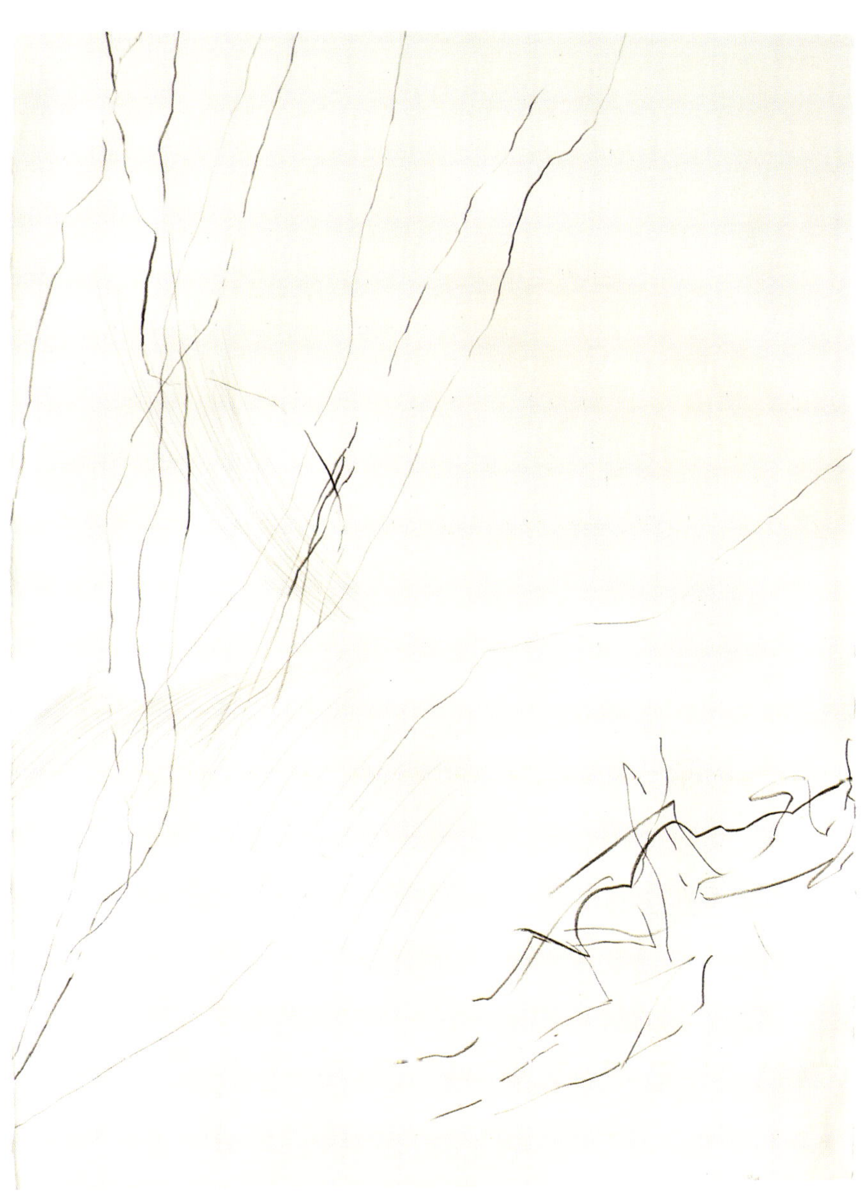

CLOUD, 8 (2008)

variously deploying the clenched delivery of charcoal strokes, the electric fluency of graphite, the streaking versatility of ink, and sometimes, all three media together. In some of these drawings, the clouds explode like supernovae; in others, they arc across the sky in quirky calligraphic sequences; in yet others, they turn into streamers or branch like broken rivers across the patchy grasslands of the mind.

Patel's cloud drawings are alive with the music of tapping and sliding strokes, calibrated between the realism of observation and the acumen of a diagram. Through their eddying and flurrying, their gathering and unravelling, the artist attends to the perennial formal problem of capturing movement and speed. The occasions of cloudness are various: exploding sprays of aerial flame greet us in some of these frames, while in others, we are soothed by passages of softness that propose thickets and hedges. Gradually, the time of viewing and the time of the clouds' passage converge: Patel's clouds are images of duration bracketed within the cosmic rhythm of irreversible change.

Each drawing works like an oscilloscope, as though it were the register of a mental situation. Some of these situations have the intimacy of mental events; others seem to hold us at a distance, a scenography of sky and mountain and forest. In crucial ways, this body of work retraces the repertoire of romantic painting that took the forces of nature as its premier subject: clouds, mountains, rivers, forests, ice floes. These are rendered, however, in pared-down, austere, yet rich near-monochrome; Patel's handling varies from a notational thread-knot-stitch briskness to opulently layered textural play.

The sky is the source of form in these drawings; but it also opens up, as though without its own knowledge, into fields and linearities from other areas of experience. There are hints of riverscapes that seem to have been scanned as satellite photographs; and we see the engraver's

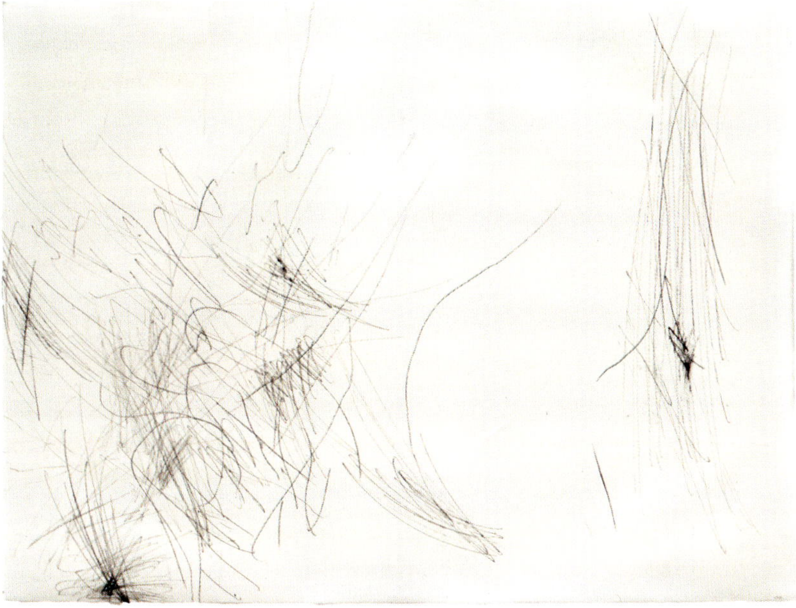

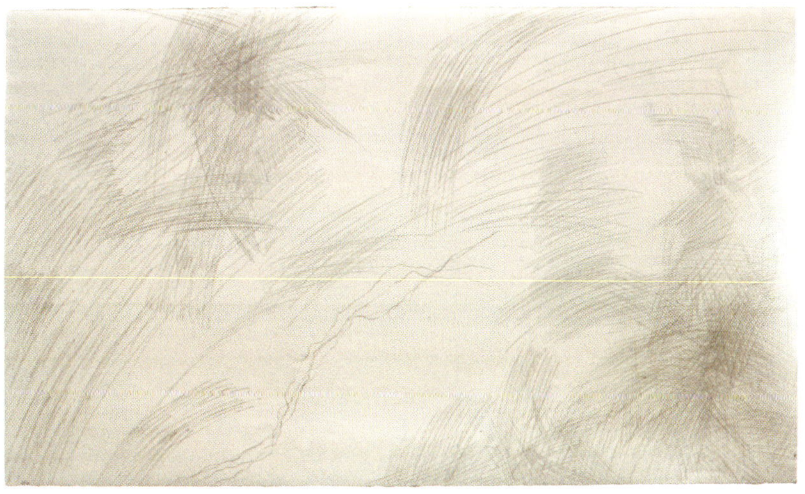

CLOUD, 6 (2008) and CLOUD, 26 (2007)

hand at work in these drawings, some of which are dominated by emptiness while others are busy with detailed line-work. Automatic writing proposes itself as a rubric in some of these works, as though the hand had been guided only by impulse, intuition, a move towards unmediated spontaneity; in some of these drawings, the traces of the marking hand remind us of events in a cloud chamber. Both in the *Wells* series and the *Clouds*, the artist has taken a turn towards abstraction: his handling freer, barely anchored in the mandate of representation, open to the suggestions of whim and chance.

As we traverse these drawings, we walk with Patel through an atlas of clouds—we think of the elaborately curlicued clouds in Buddhist thangkas, of the clouds in Mantegna's skies and Tiepolo's, and of the classificatory efforts of the nineteenth-century amateur scientist Luke Howard, who first applied to the clouds the scientific names by which we now know them. To cross the field of clouds is to look up and be gathered into a cosmic theatre of arrivals and departures: the true inward and philosophical theme of these drawings is the impermanence of form.

IV. The Memory of Skulls

Patel executed seven charcoal drawings of skulls during a six-week period in 2010, each rendered in a single sitting. In these drawings, Patel memorializes the paradoxical vividness of life's aftermath. Using three grades of charcoal—hard, medium and soft—he contours the skull through a variation of densities, rather than effecting a straightforward volumetric presentation. Each skull is caressed, not chiselled into being: each displays a slight but unmistakeable ghosting, seeming to rock or shift in a blank space that becomes activated by this movement. If Patel has returned to the disciplines of the anatomy class at medical school (he was trained as

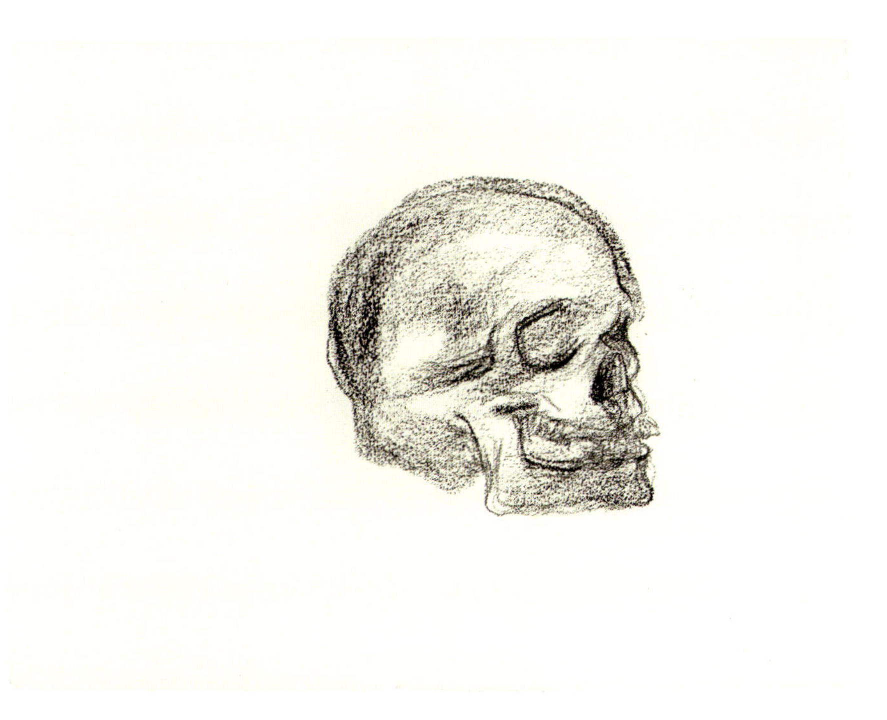

(ABOVE and FOLLOWING PAGES) SKULL, 1–7 (2010)

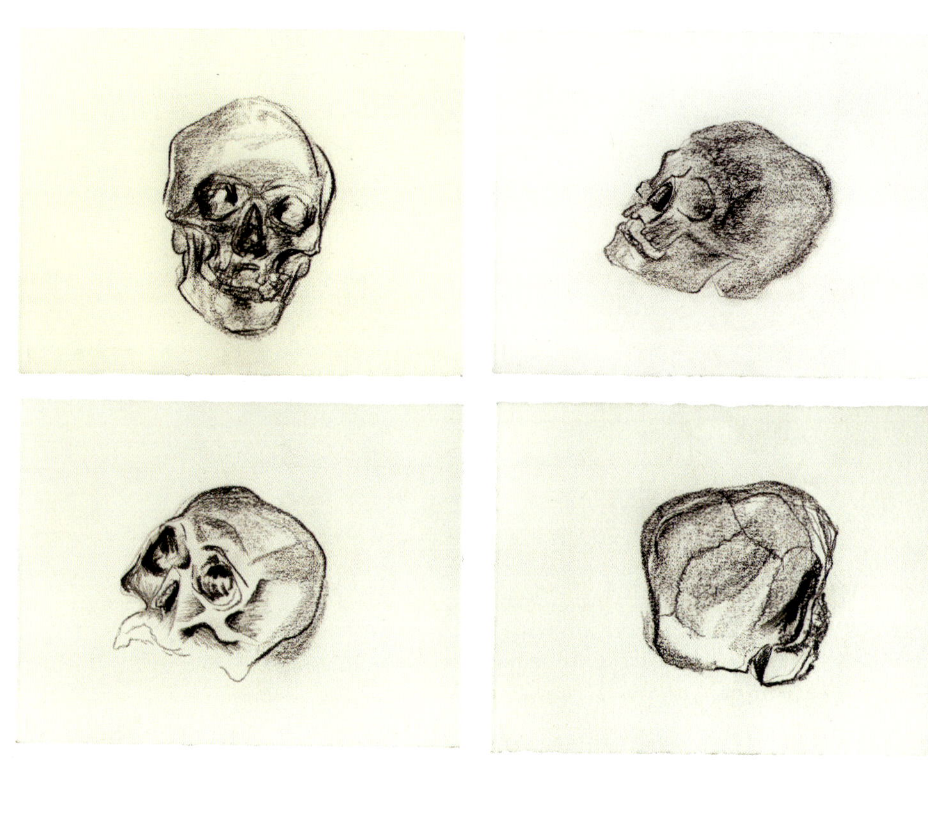

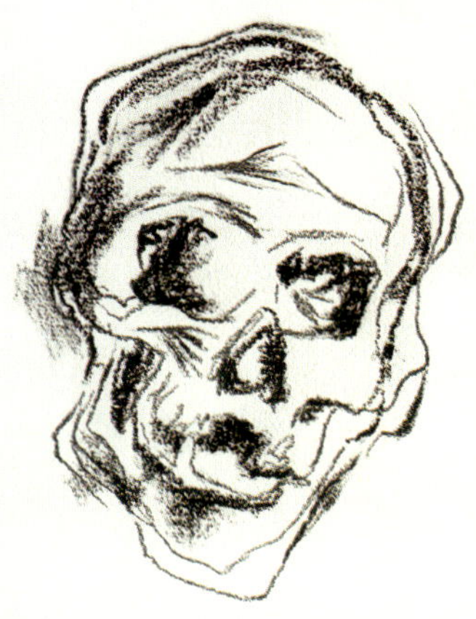

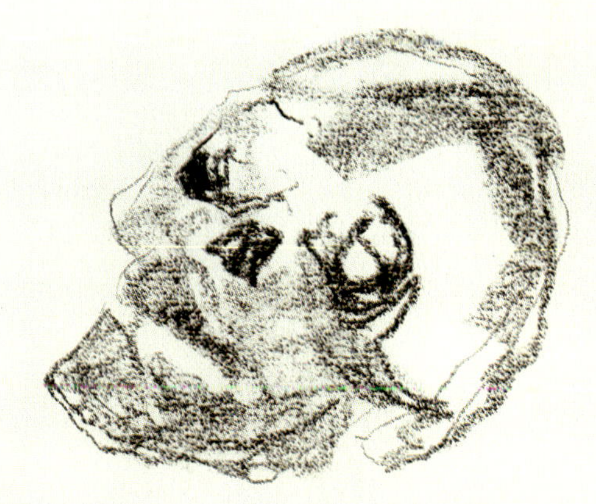

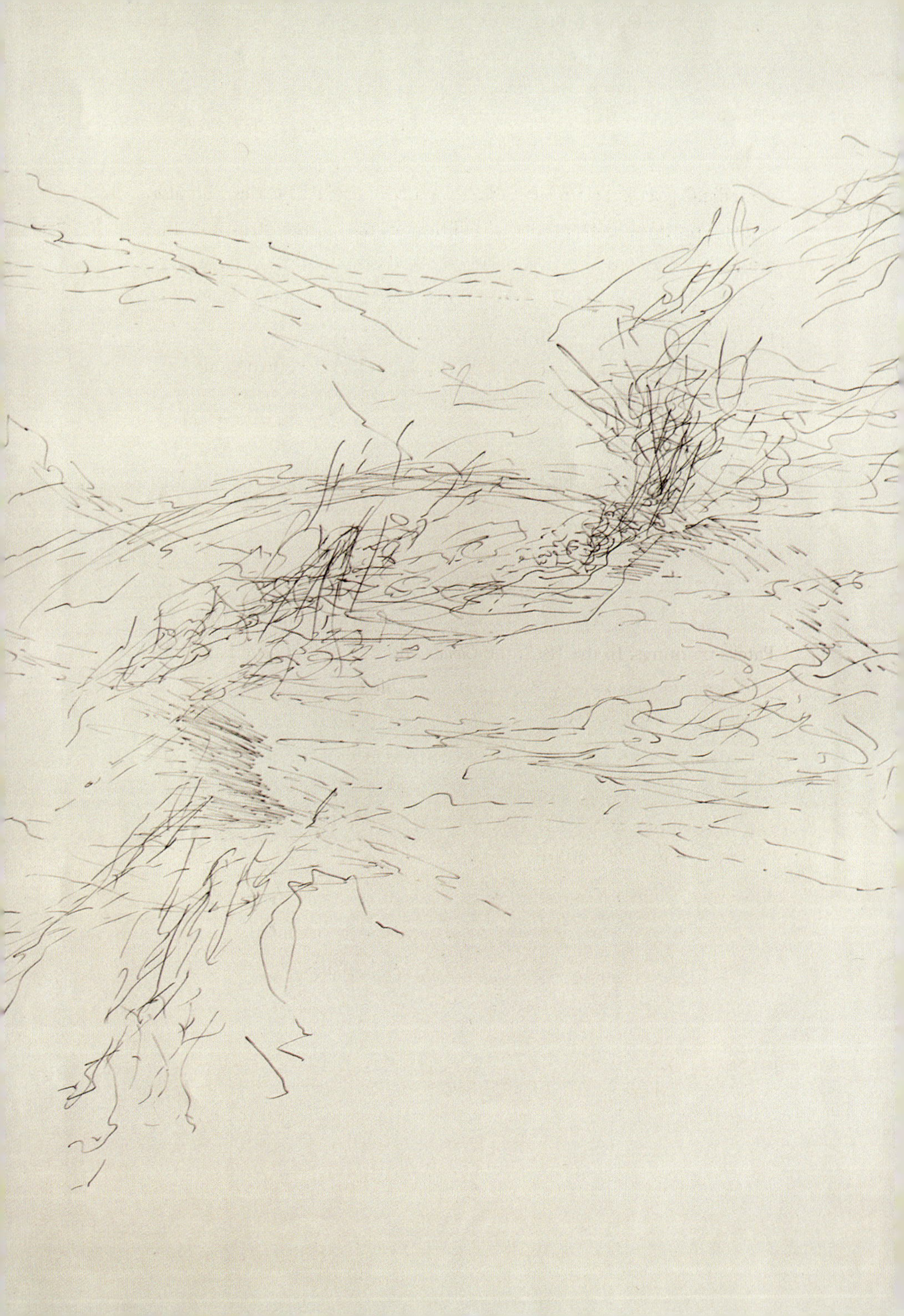

a medical doctor and practised as such for several decades), he also derives propulsion from the visualities of the comic strip and the animation film here. Far from losing the authority that the dress of flesh confers, these skulls gain a new and oracular masterfulness. Calibrated between artefact and spirit, these are not mere evidentiary relics of the past, but portraits of impulse, regret, satiety and repose. Before our eyes, the object becomes a presence; the presence, a portent.

These are intensely emotive works: they register the ravages of time, space, circumstance. They sing of the processes by which bone is cracked and fissured like the earth that holds it, by which it becomes one with sand, wind, earth, starfish and darkness, as it bleaches into spectrality. To my mind, these are speaking skulls: oracles, voice-presences and skeletal remains of the battered, marginal, dissident protagonists of many of Patel's paintings. In the *Wells*, the *Clouds* and the *Skulls*, Gieve Patel subjects the promise of elsewhere and the afterlife to intense scrutiny. What appears to fascinate him now is not the figure as the passionate articulation of an individual and social history, but the invisible traces that we leave on our environment as we make our passage through a place and a period, and the equivocal traces that we leave behind us to mark that passage, hostages abandoned to the interpretative kindness of those who will follow.

Bombay

April 2011

Notes

1   Sudhir Patwardhan, 'Gieve Patel: Looking into a Well . . . beyond Metaphor', reprinted in *Gieve Patel + Sudhir Patwardhan* (New York: Bose Pacia/ BP Contemporary Art of India Series, VOL. 28, 2006), p. 20.

2   Patwardhan, 'Gieve Patel: Looking into a Well', p. 20.

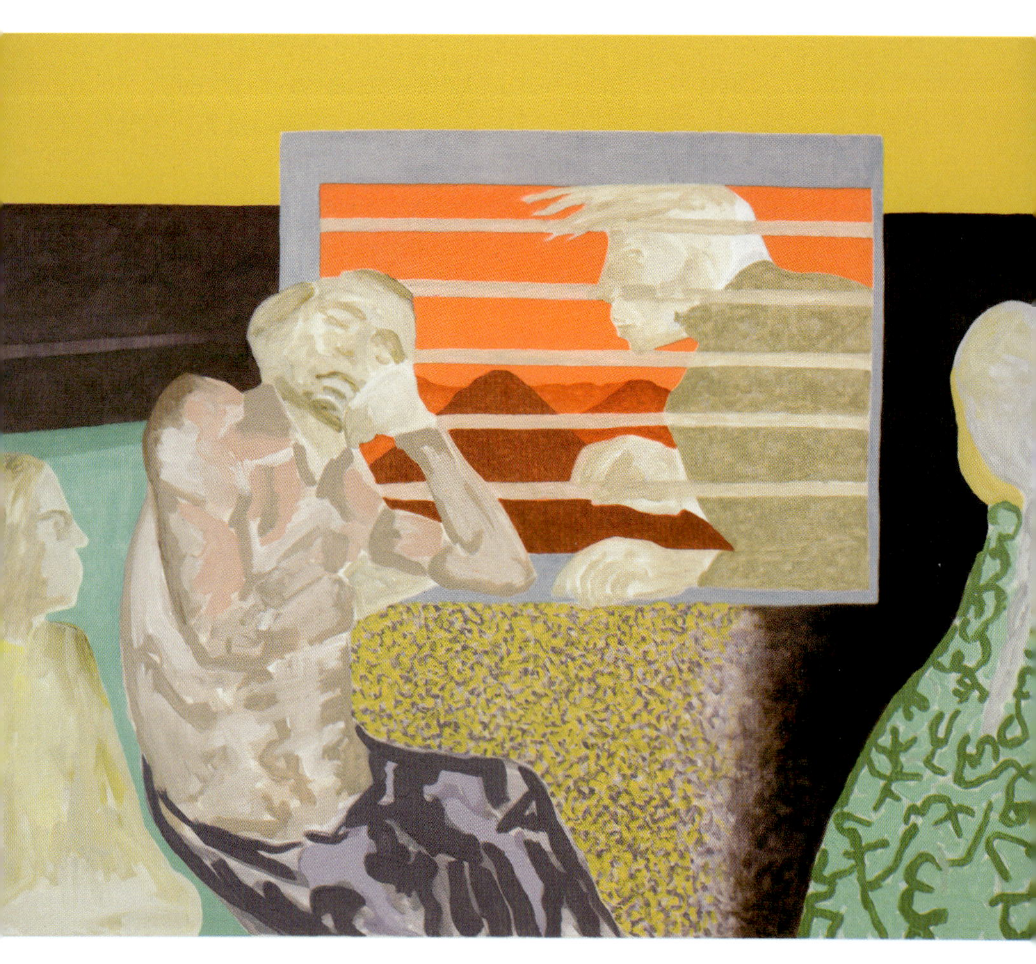

FOOTBOARD RIDER (2016)

6.

Crossing the Bridge of Paradox

> The city like a passion burns.
> He dreams of morning walks, alone,
> And floating on a wave of sand.
> But still his mind its traffic turns
> Away from beach and tree and stone
> To kindred clamour close at hand.
>
> –Nissim Ezekiel, 'Urban'

I.

The 14 works gathered to form Gieve Patel's current exhibition, *Footboard Rider*, offer renewed testimony to the artist's lifelong preoccupation with the marginal, vulnerable or extreme figure, taken from the sidelines of society or from unbearable intensities of experience, and set at the centre of his paintings. Whether it is the man struggling against the rain, the maimed beggar, the eunuch, the mutilated body on a beach or the martyr at the stake, Patel's figures are clothed in the robust specificity of their social milieu or historical circumstances. They are modelled on individuals the artist has encountered in the street, the public garden, the clinic, or the wharf; or else, they have been culled from his passionate engagement with the history of painting and cinema. Despite this seeming recognizability, Patel's figures remain enigmatic. They are never so distant as to be alien to us, of course; yet they are never so close as to be neutralized by familiarity. And while they can sometimes be insistently material and present, they can also be spectral, suggestive of apparitions.

The protagonist of this exhibition's title painting is one of Patel's more spectral dramatis personae. He inhabits a threshold between the contained interior of a commuter or long-distance train—a mobile habitat familiar to the denizens of the artist's home city, Bombay—and the landscape seen outside its window, all red hills and orange sky. Are we inside the train, looking out at the footboard rider, we ask ourselves? Or are we outside the train, looking in? The construction of the painting subtly disorients our viewerly certainties.

In the same way, Patel's long-term fascination with the moment of looking into a well, and with the passage of clouds in the sky, opens us to cosmic intimations. In these works, the artist pulls away from the figure, hinting at a transcendence of the bodied self; or perhaps, more accurately, at the possibility of such a transcendence. For Patel's wells are sensuously conceived: his haptic attentiveness embraces the textures of stone, brick, loam, vegetation, water in flow and at rest; he does not isolate his wells, miraculous as they are, from the cycles of human activity and utility indicated by the winch, well head or other architectural features that are occasionally reflected in their surfaces. It is possible, also, to read the floating world of the well as an image of the mind, with thoughts, sensations and impulses striating and succeeding one another on its mercurial surface. Equally, it might suggest the millennial cycles of gathering and dispersal through which the universe maps its life cycle.

In this sense, Patel's wells bear a considerable affinity with his graphite, charcoal and ink studies of clouds: natural ephemera approximated through the graphic gesture, which remind us of the interplay between mortality and eternity within which we shape our lives. Patel's artistic project is that of taking up a quotidian moment, so naturalized and rendered routine that it no longer attracts attention, and to visit a transfiguration upon it: to make it mysterious and radiant, marked by an otherness that invites us to look more closely at all that remains unexamined in our lives.

II.

In theatre, an actor finds his or her place on stage through a script, or through a sequence of moves plotted and blocked, or even, in more experimental situations, through evolving relationships with other actors sharing the experience of performance. By contrast, Patel often declines to offer the protagonists who people his paintings a definite script, or to orchestrate the precise relationships that hold them together. As viewers, we find ourselves reaching intuitively for the currents and sediments of affect in his obliquely told tales. We gauge the degrees of familiarity and estrangement from the everyday that he layers into his art, as we attempt to interpret the true inwardness of his tableaux. Our interpretations are, of course, subject to change; they shift as our perceptions shift to accommodate allusions, shades of meaning, undercurrents, the utterances and the silences of these paintings and drawings. Elsewhere, I have written of how 'Patel's paintings often feature groups that are the interwoven sum of unspoken privacies' and the 'content of Patel's compressed narratives remains unspelled-out, withheld as in the paintings of Piero della Francesca, whom he admires.'[1]

In this spirit, let us approach *Footboard Rider* and *Embrace* (both 2016). The first work thrums with the momentum of an expanding metropolis and a sprawling subcontinent; it takes its place in a decades-long itinerary

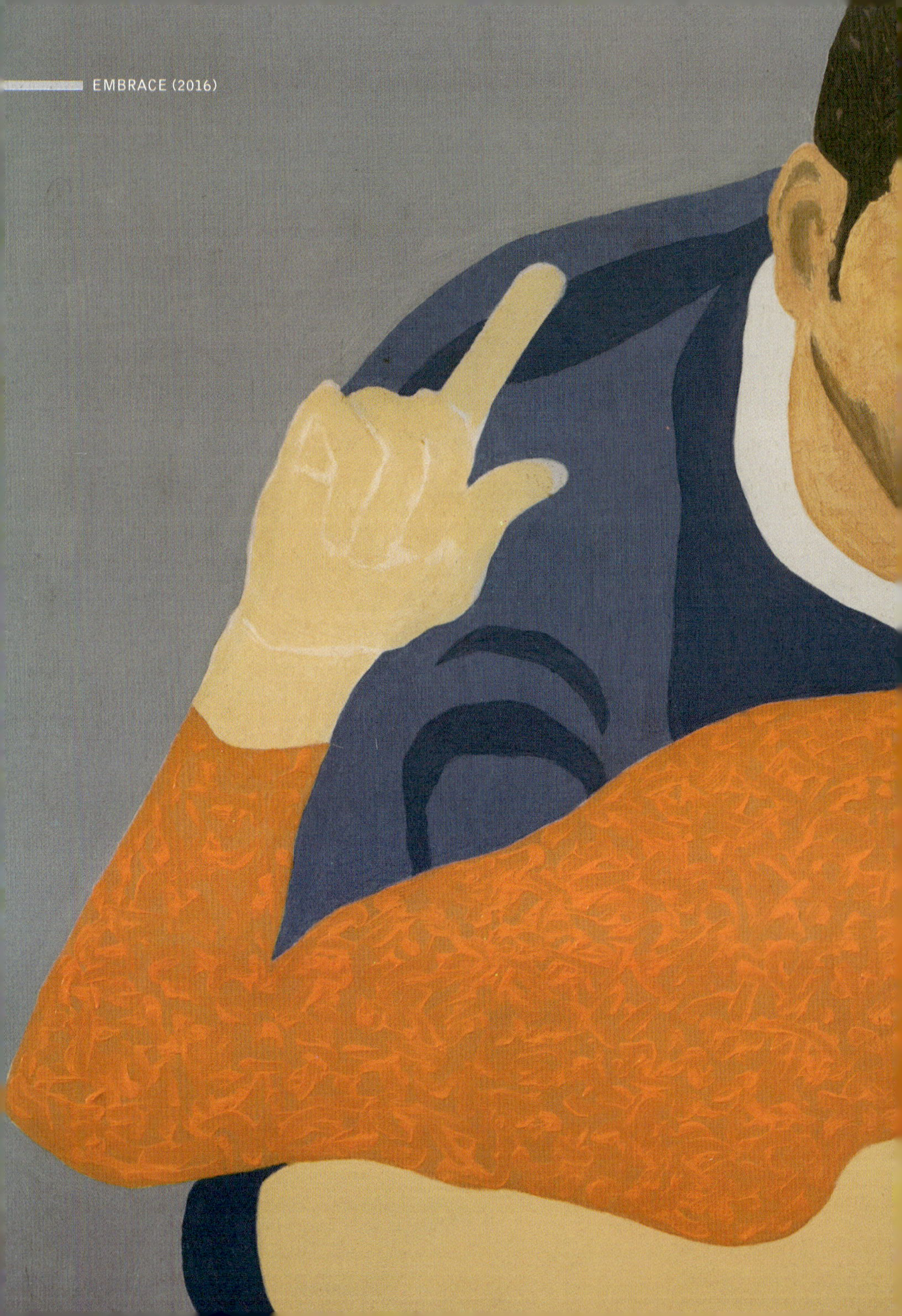

EMBRACE (2016)

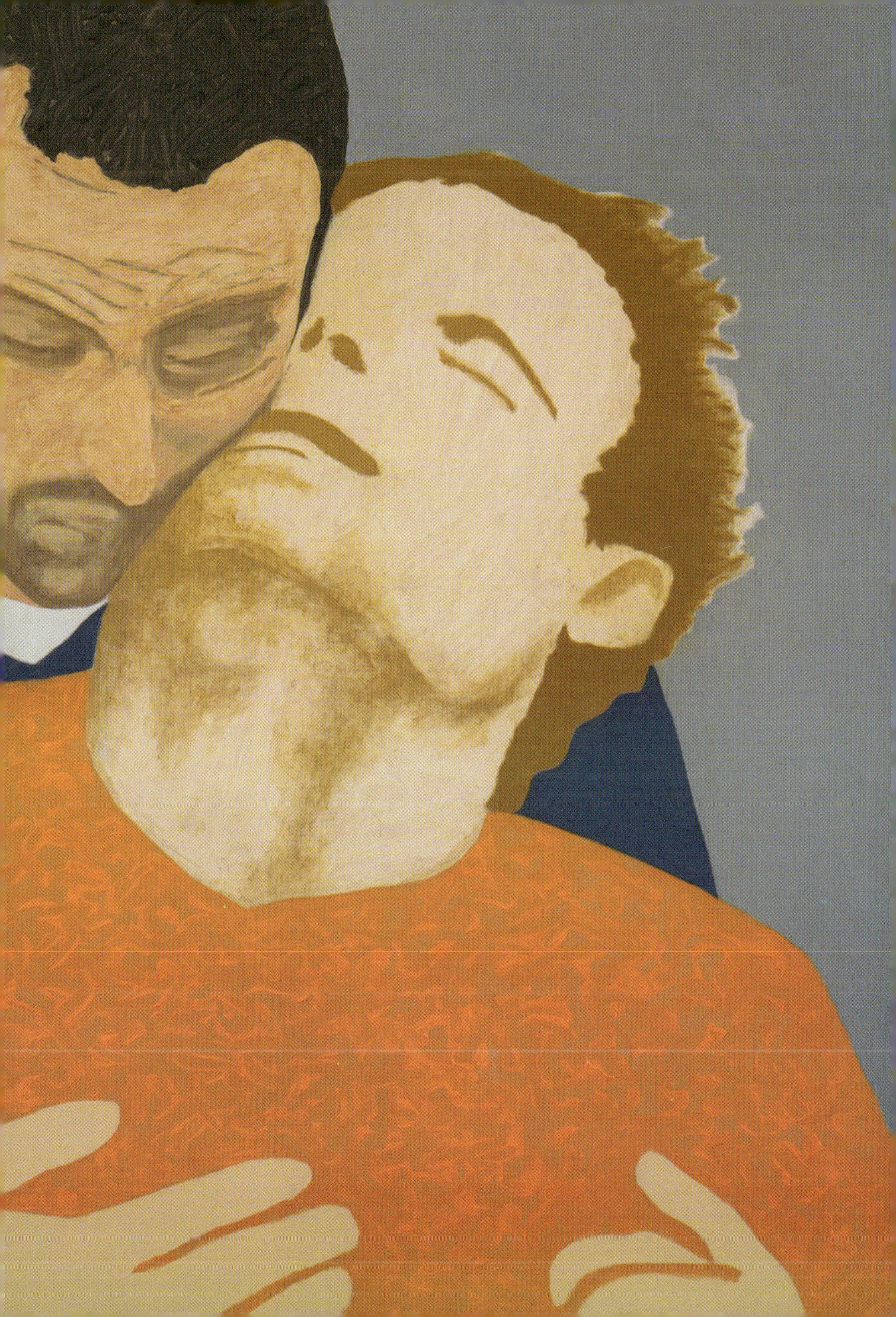

of paintings in which Patel has invoked the environs of the train station, the deserted railway platform, the figure of the porter, and the early-morning train ride. In some of these paintings, especially of the early and mid-1970s—*Lighted Platform* (1973) and *Figure in Landscape* (1976) come to mind—space was as persuasive a protagonist as any human figure. The second work is inspired by the newspaper photograph of a pivotal moment in a football match. This, too, may be contextualized within a research and preparatory practice of the artist's, which involves the use of media photographs, seen to particular advantage in a series from the late 1960s and early 1970s devoted to the figure of the politician, including *Dead Politician* (1969) and *Conference Table* (1972).

Footboard Rider is dominated, visually, by the eponymous wraith-like figure: he seems to be hanging out of the train, his hair punked by the wind, his stance and aspect those of a highwayman boarding a stage coach or a duellist challenging invisible powers to combat. Inside the compartment of the train, heading either to Bombay's suburbs or to distant hinterland towns, are other figures, one of them lost to sleep; outside the window, the vista is resplendent with the colours of dawn or twilight. The painting holds out multiple surprises. The orange and red of the landscape are projective colours, played against the grain here to recessive effect; meanwhile, the brushy mustard-gamboge surface of the train interior shades off into darkness. The longer we look at the painting, the more we are drawn into its reverie-like mood, and the less certain we grow of our bearings. The train's interior begins to resemble its exterior; we cannot tell where sunrise ends and dusk begins, or where inside passes into outside. And the footboard rider: is he real, within the framework of the painting, or is he simply a phantasm in a dream that has possessed the sleeping figure?

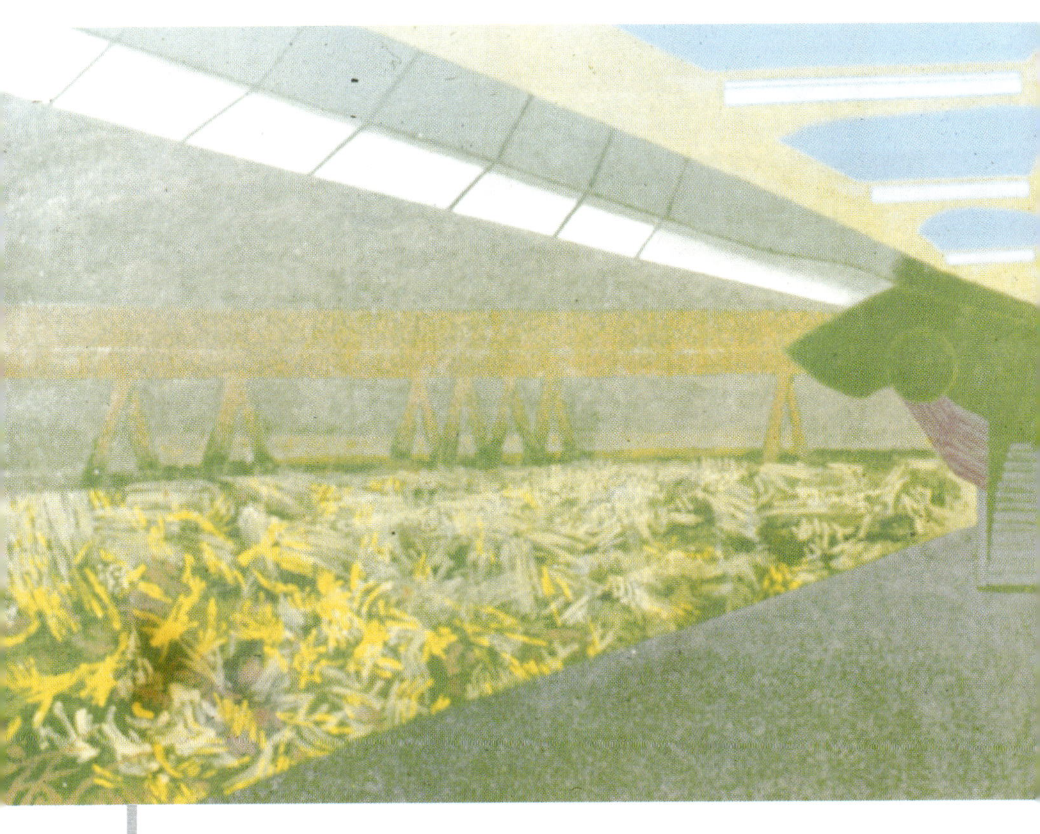

LIGHTED PLATFORM (1973)

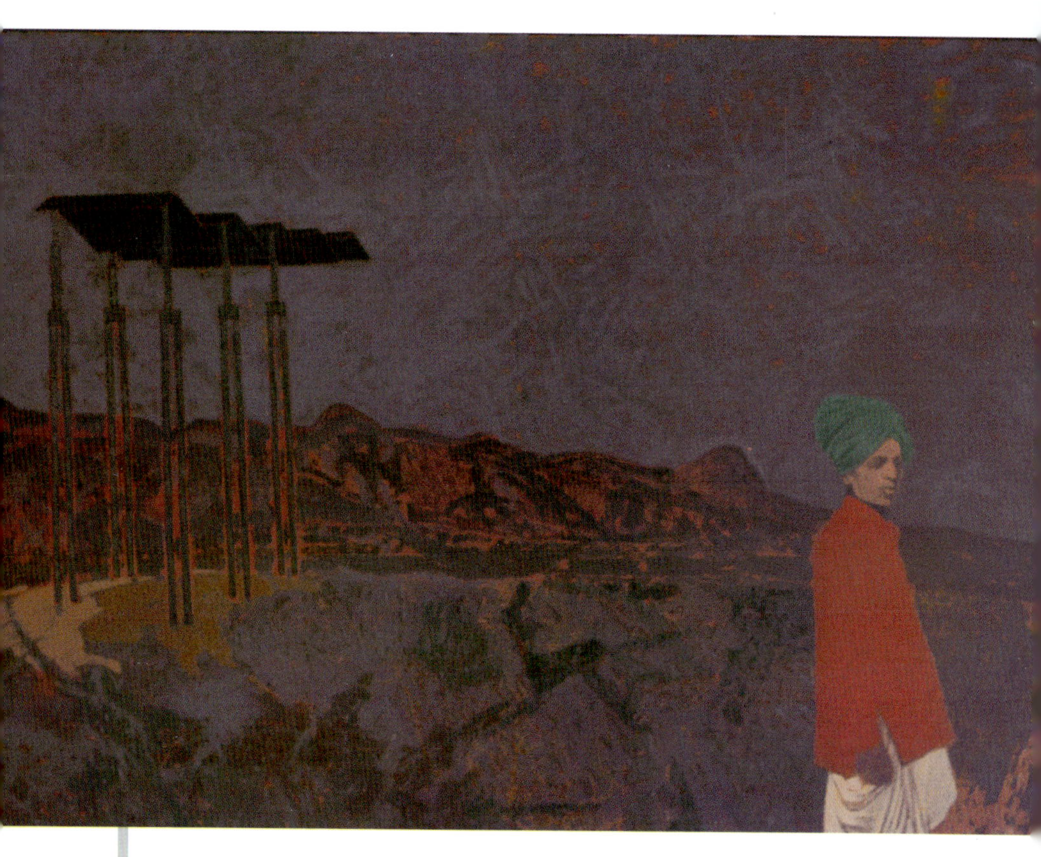

FIGURE IN LANDSCAPE (1976)

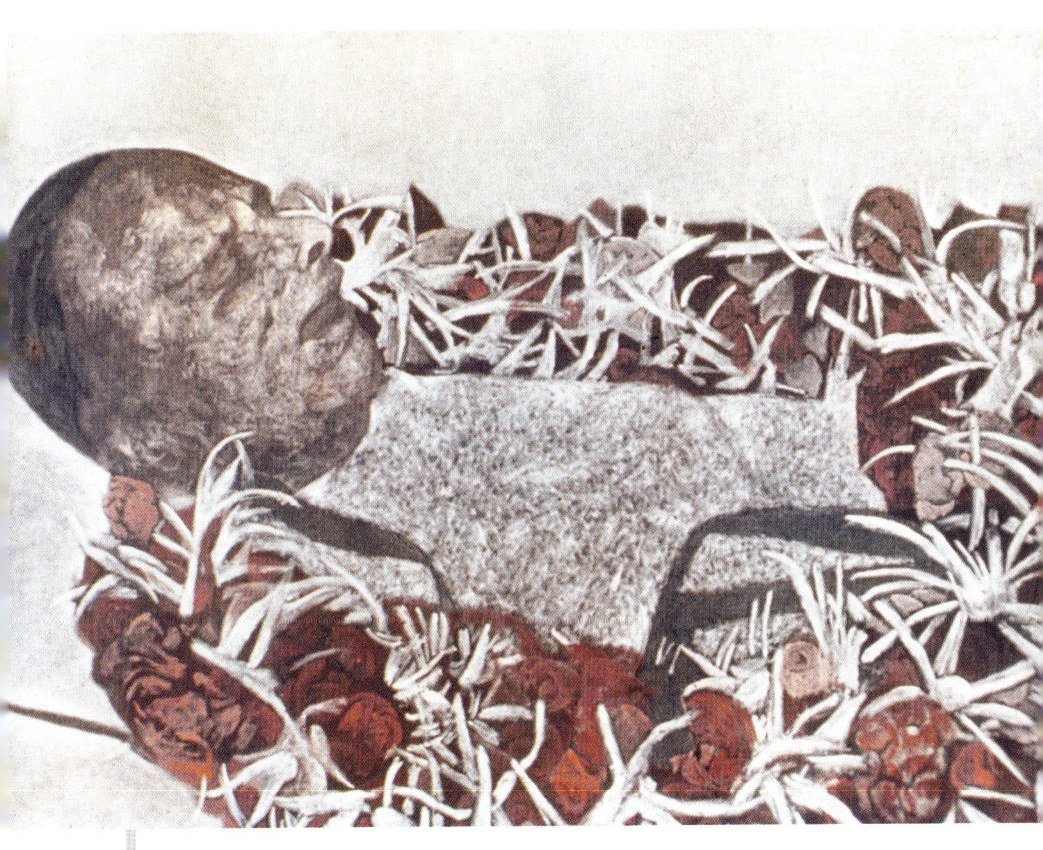

DEAD POLITICIAN (1969)

Embrace is a deeply moving, even holy work—and I use the latter adjective advisedly. In the first instant of viewing, we sense that we stand in the presence of a drama larger than ourselves: a drama at once unfolding in the moment and perennial in the manner in which it is likely to repeat itself in a universal structure of events. What do we feel, when we look at these two male figures, both strong: one, in orange, apparently falling or struck down, gesturing for attention as he communicates something of urgency to the other, in blue, who holds him tenderly, offering comfort or consolation, bending to hear him so that their cheeks touch? There is a tragic heroism to these figures, veined with an unabashedly masculine solidarity that could be read, perhaps quite persuasively, as homoerotic kinship.

I describe the atmosphere of this painting as 'holy' because it is charged with a sense of exaltation, of communion, of intimate exchange transmuted into sacred moment. Are these men, perhaps, a martyred saint and his apostle? Has one been betrayed, and is the other the only survivor from the shipwreck of trust? Are we bearing witness, here, to a rite of succession? Is the man in orange pointing upward to indicate an annunciation of things to come, a revelation of what has been occluded, or a last word of counsel?

Embrace is resonant with intimations of the trecento in the tenor of its subject, its tonality, its exaltation, and the importance of gesture. Here, as elsewhere, in his oeuvre, Patel demonstrates the fascinating extent to which he has internalized the legacies of the Italian Primitives, the Dutch and Flemish masters, and the pioneers of the Northern Renaissance. To him, Giotto, Rogier van der Weyden and Matthias Grünewald are not merely references to be plucked for citation; rather, with their capacity to invoke an entire lifeworld or habitus of emotions, they have become indwelling and definitive elements of his artistic temperament.

III.

The figure assumes varied avatars in Patel's work; and as I write that sentence, I correct myself, stop myself from setting an idealist misconception afloat. For there is no a priori, archetypal, universal template from which Patel develops his particular figures; on the contrary, it is from the materiality, the diverse granularity and specificity of his protagonists that we may establish, following Wittgenstein, a 'family resemblance' which connects them through gradations of overlap rather than unvarying identity.[2] If *Footboard Rider* attends to the phantasmal figure and *Embrace* to figures in a state of exaltation, another grouping of works in this exhibition articulates the artist's continuing engagement with the body as hostage to time, to the processes of attrition, decay and extinction that time enacts on the flesh. *Meditations on Old Age* (2013), a group of four paintings, *Mourners* (2005), a group of three, and *Dawn Elegy* (2017)—all carry into the present that preoccupation with the vulnerable, wounded, abandoned, ravaged and heartbreakingly mortal body which lay at the core of Patel's *Gallery of Man* series, inaugurated in the early 1980s.

In these recent entries in the catalogue of the *Gallery of Man*, we—or, at any rate, I—detect an intriguing shift of attitude. While formerly, as with *Crushed Head* and *Drowned Woman* (both 1984), the gravitas of the portraiture evoked our sorrow, pity and horror, it seems to me that Patel's studies of ageing and of lamentation now communicate a complex tension between two apparently mutually contradictory responses to the human subject. The first chromatic reality that hits us, when we look at *Meditations on Old Age*, is that these are bright paintings, defined by an almost DayGlo palette of yellows, purples and greens. Is that an apparatchik from Mao's China, or a man in a wig with a very marked side part? Is the man with glasses set in a purple frame an ageing rock star, or was he merely caught in strange cross-lights? And that body with its

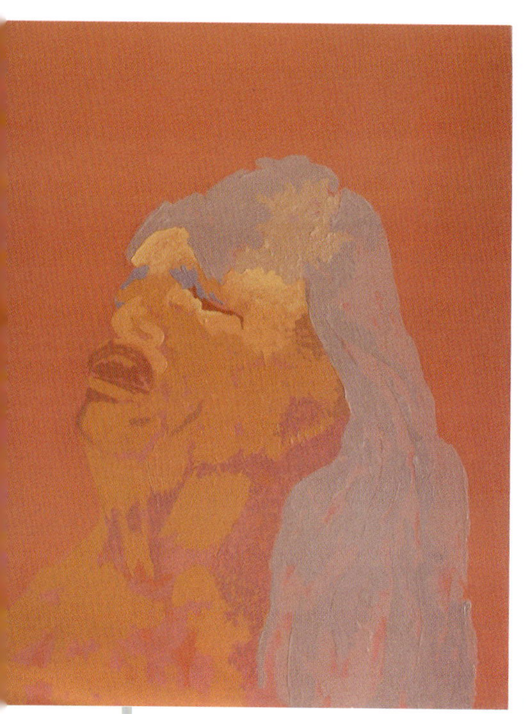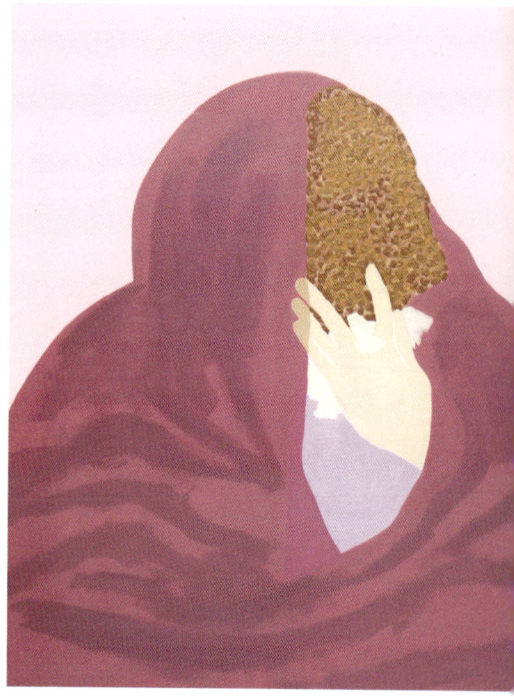

MOURNER, 1 and 3 (ABOVE LEFT and RIGHT) and MOURNER, 2 (FACING PAGE) (2005)

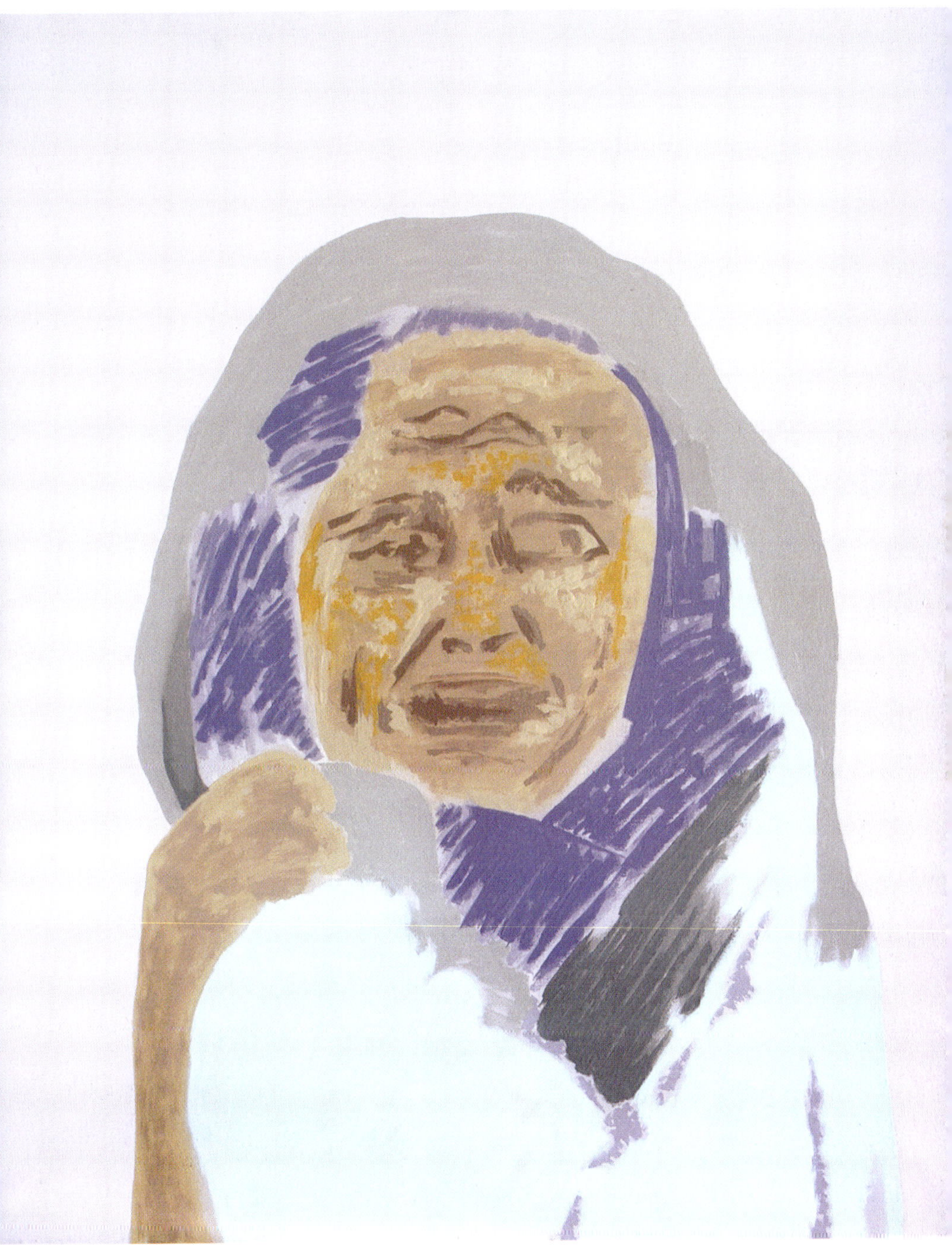

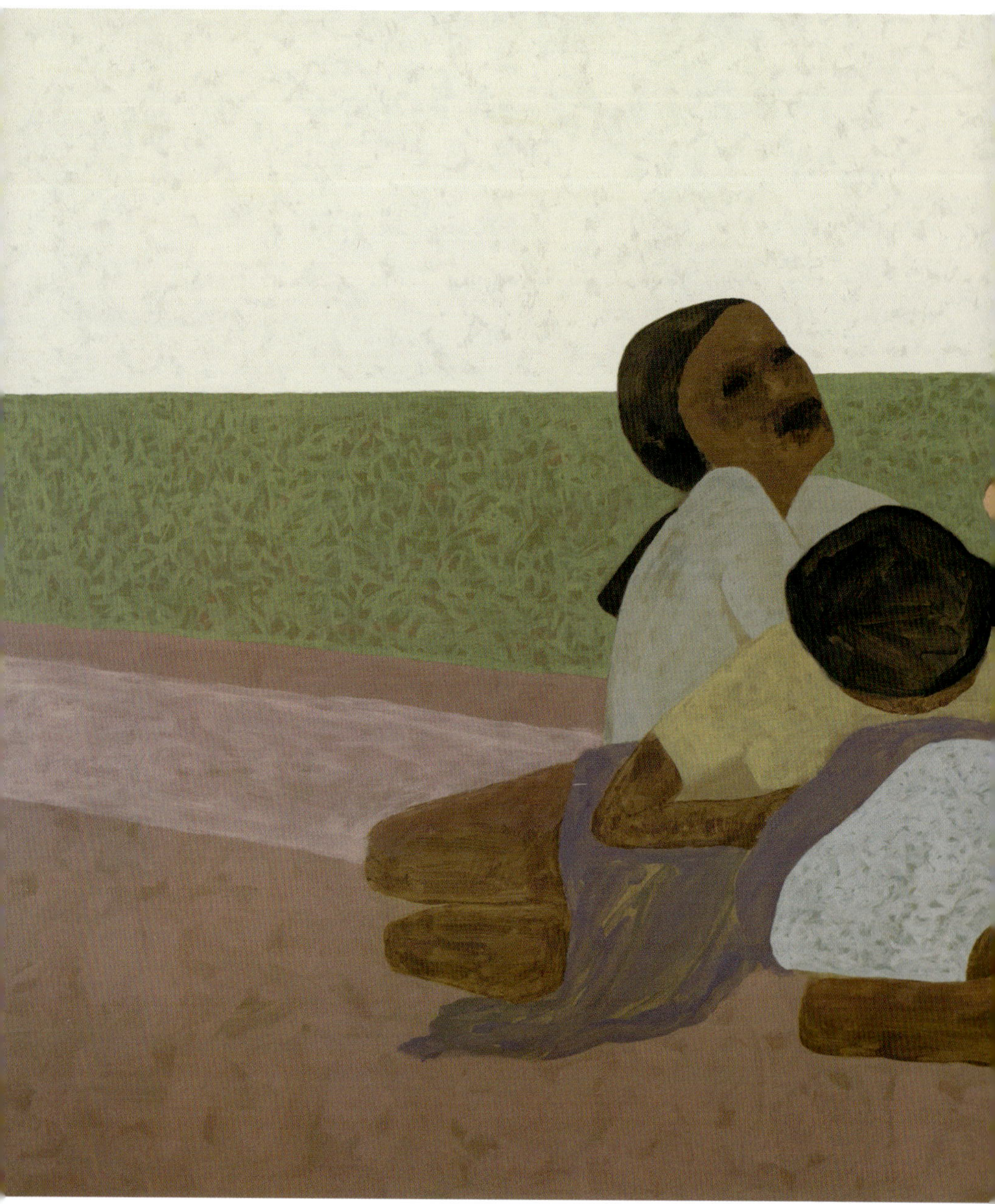

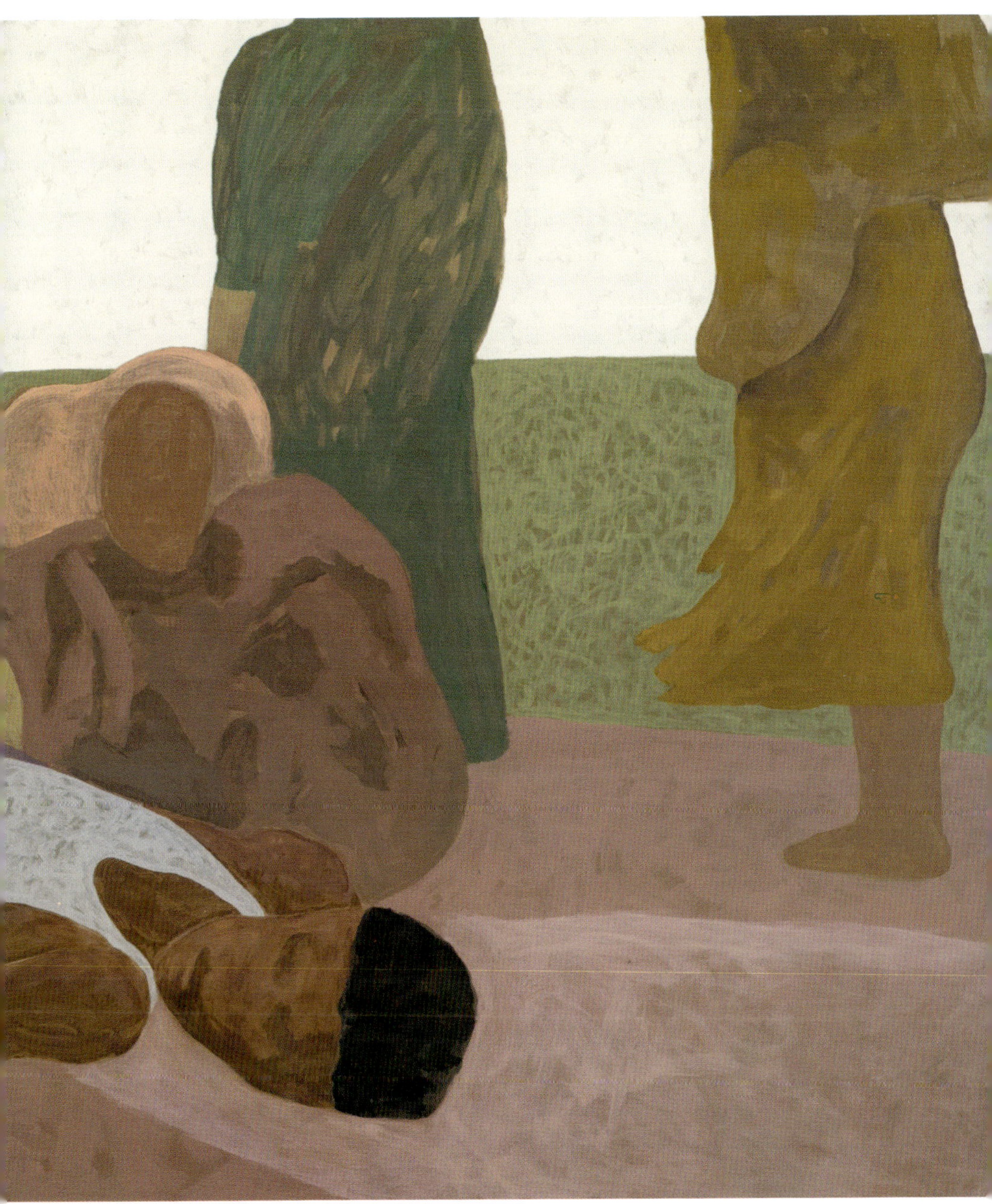

DAWN ELEGY (2017)

luminous yellows and shades of pink, a riff on Patel's *Battered Man in Land-scape* (1993), why does it indicate vitality even as it seems to have suffered untold depredation?

One answer may well be that Patel has chosen, now, to present a collision between inevitable decline and resurgent vitality, taking a cue from Dylan Thomas' ringing demand that old age should not 'go gentle into that good night', that it should 'rage, rage against the dying of the light'. But the chromatic sumptuousness of the *Meditations on Old Age*, and the palpable vibrancy of their brush strokes, so festively at odds with their ostensible subject matter, could also indicate another clash of instincts: on the one hand, the artist's long-standing philanthropic releasement of the self towards others, through empathy; and on the other, a previously less evident misanthropic impulse, alert to the foibles of the precariously perched survivor, asserting itself through gentle, carnivalesque mockery.

In *Mourners*, three paintings whose putative sitters suggest the members of a dispersed chorus, it is the philanthropic impulse that prevails. Based on graphite studies made by Patel in 1971, these paintings communicate various registers of grief, from the first moment of seemingly insuperable shock to the stylized manifestation of loss almost as rapture, as threnody, as song. Empathy, again, is the deep-welling ground note of *Dawn Elegy*: it is a group portrait strongly imbued with the mythic freight of a deposition, translated into the demotic ordinariness of a city street, with a dead man lying on the asphalt while his family surrounds him. The lives of the group have been shaken forever by an event of catastrophic proportions; that is the focus of this work, and not the lightly implied truth that the cycles of metropolitan life, as embodied by the pedestrians standing about, will continue regardless.

IV.

With the graphite and charcoal triptych, *Joan of Arc (after Carl Dreyer)* (2016), Patel wrestles with the larger-than-life figure of the martyr, the heroine turned victim, the saint burned at the stake as a blasphemer and heretic. Here we have the figure in extreme conditions, visualized as, successively, under threat of imminent extinction, violently extinguished, and then reduced to ashes. The artist's point of departure, for this triptych, is the silent-era black-and-white cinematic classic, *The Passion of Joan of Arc* (1928), directed by Danish filmmaker Carl Theodor Dreyer. *The Passion* was noted for its remarkable lighting, which harshly contoured the actors' features and the architecture of the concrete set that represented the mediaeval prison in Rouen where an ecclesiastical kangaroo court presided over Joan of Arc's trial in 1431. Dreyer's film emphasized the use of close-up and low-angle shots, imparting a disquieting emotional intensity to his narrative and the experience of viewing it.

Patel's electric line—familiar from his continuing series of drawings of clouds—is pressed into highly effective service here, to achieve a variety of effects evocative of the solitary figure of the dissident being stigmatized and offered up as human sacrifice, the charred body memorialized in residues of ash and calcinated bone while the seemingly evanescent spirit endures as aura, as the afterlife of story. *Joan of Arc (after Carl Dreyer)* reminds us, also, of Patel's lifelong preoccupation with finding painterly or graphic solutions to the formal question of how to represent plasma and lamina: fire, water, smoke and steam.

V.

Patel's fascination with the problem of painting water—how to render transparency by palpable means?—animates his continuing series of

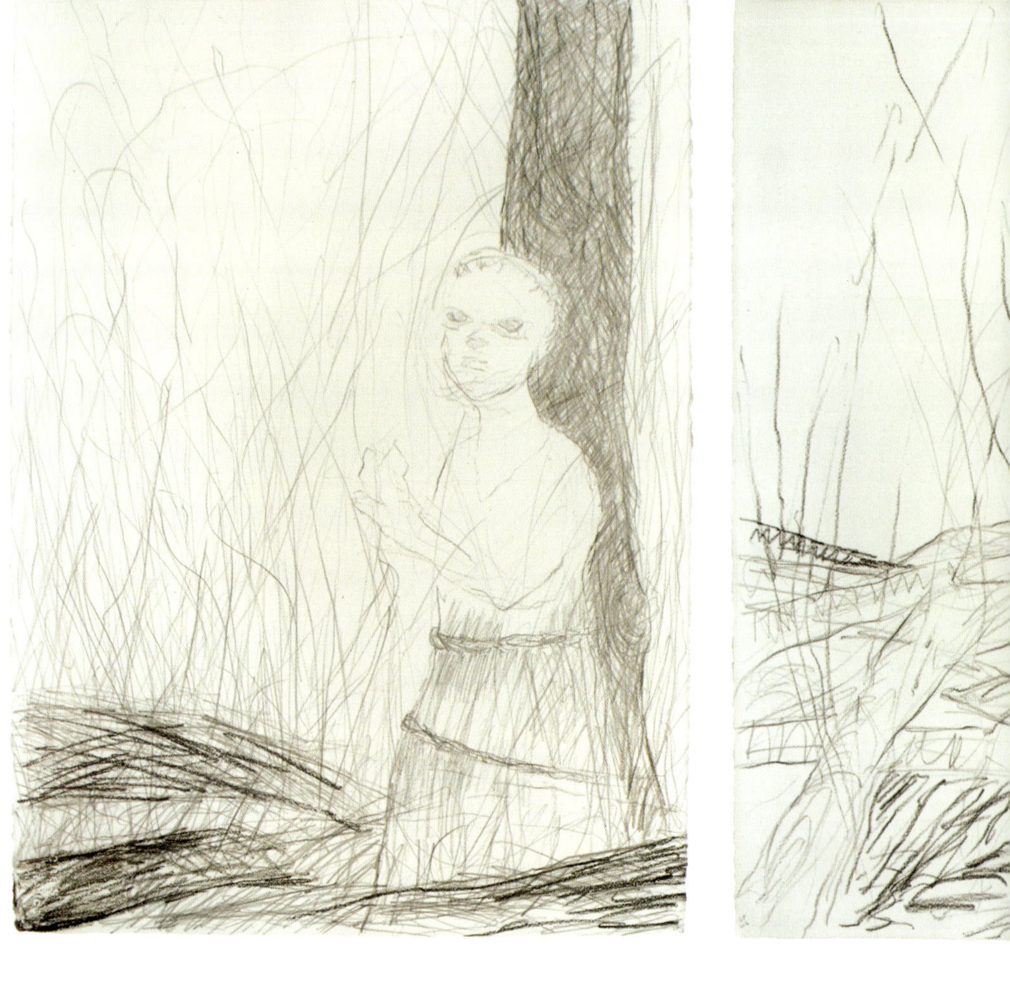

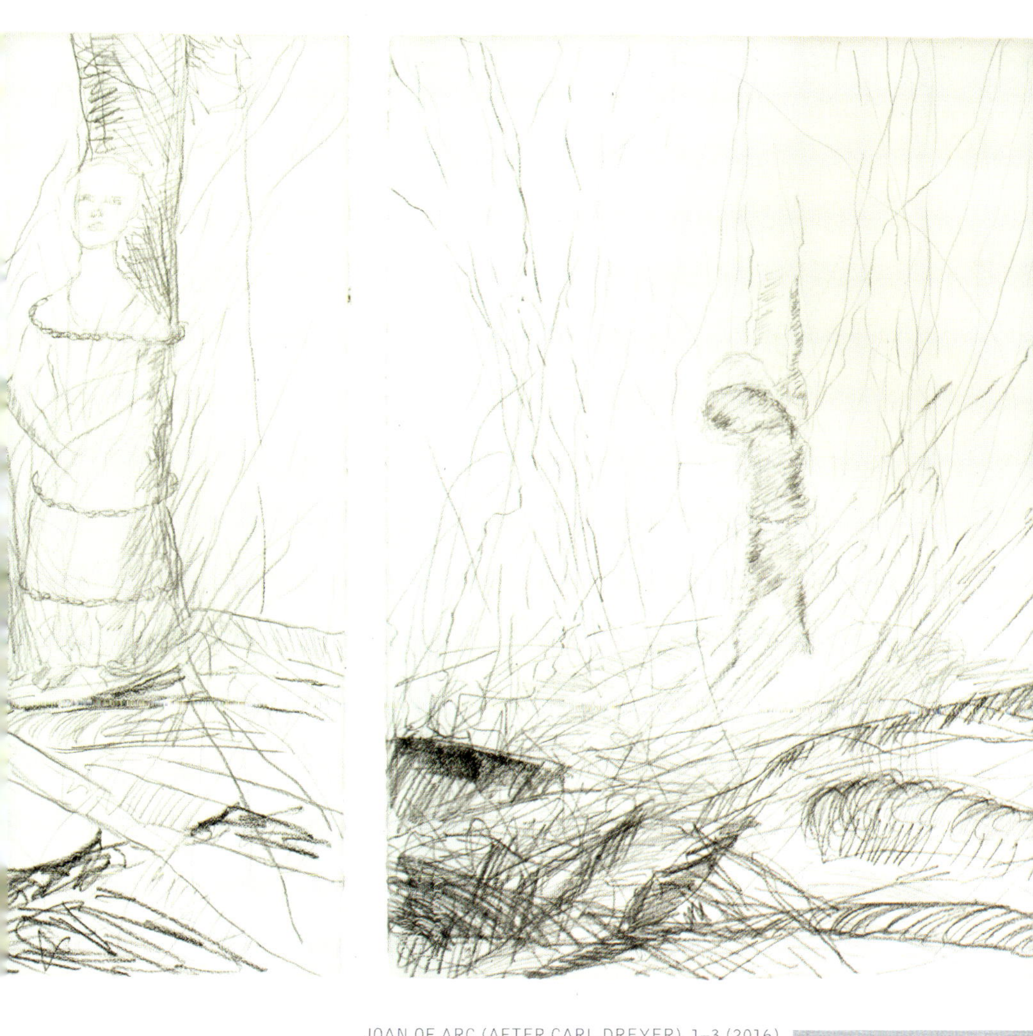

JOAN OF ARC (AFTER CARL DREYER), 1–3 (2016)

paintings titled *Looking into a Well*, of which there are now nearly 25. Formally, these wells enable Patel to express his abstractionist energies; at the related conceptual level, they permit him to voice his receptiveness to a numinous transcendental vision that embraces yet exceeds the conditions of material existence. Elsewhere, I have written of how, in such works, his 'preferred texture, a quirky, mottled tapestry, signifies a myriad teemingness redolent of microscopic life while also suggesting a fluid connection among all beings and things.'[3]

The temporality of Patel's wells varies between the momentary scale of ephemeral effects and the geological scale of eternity. These wells invite us to undertake journeys into other worlds: *Looking into a Well: A Spray of Blossoms* (2010) is an atlas in microcosm, with the drifting, iridescent forms of flowers ablaze across it; *Looking into a Well: Evening Dazzle* (2014) invites us into the life of algae, moss, stone and exposed brick at sunset; *Looking into a Well: Four Pillars* (2015), with its trailing chain of clouds and the architecture reflected in its water, prompts us to dwell on the nature of reflection, on whether we are looking at a mirror or a channel here. Significantly, we realize that we always look at rather than down into Patel's wells: an experience that would have been perpendicularly oriented in life is framed parallel to us in art. Might we regard these wells as portholes that make us intimate yet distanced witnesses to another domain? Or do they sometimes act as mandalas, cosmic images, restful yet alive to the world's unease?

Like the protagonist of Nissim Ezekiel's 'Urban', which gives this essay its epigraph, Gieve Patel has nurtured close, productive relationships both with the city and the small town or village; with the realm of natural forces and the realm of human relationships. No captive of a banal either-orism of illusory choice, his blood is quickened both by 'beach and tree and stone' as well as by 'kindred clamour close at hand'.

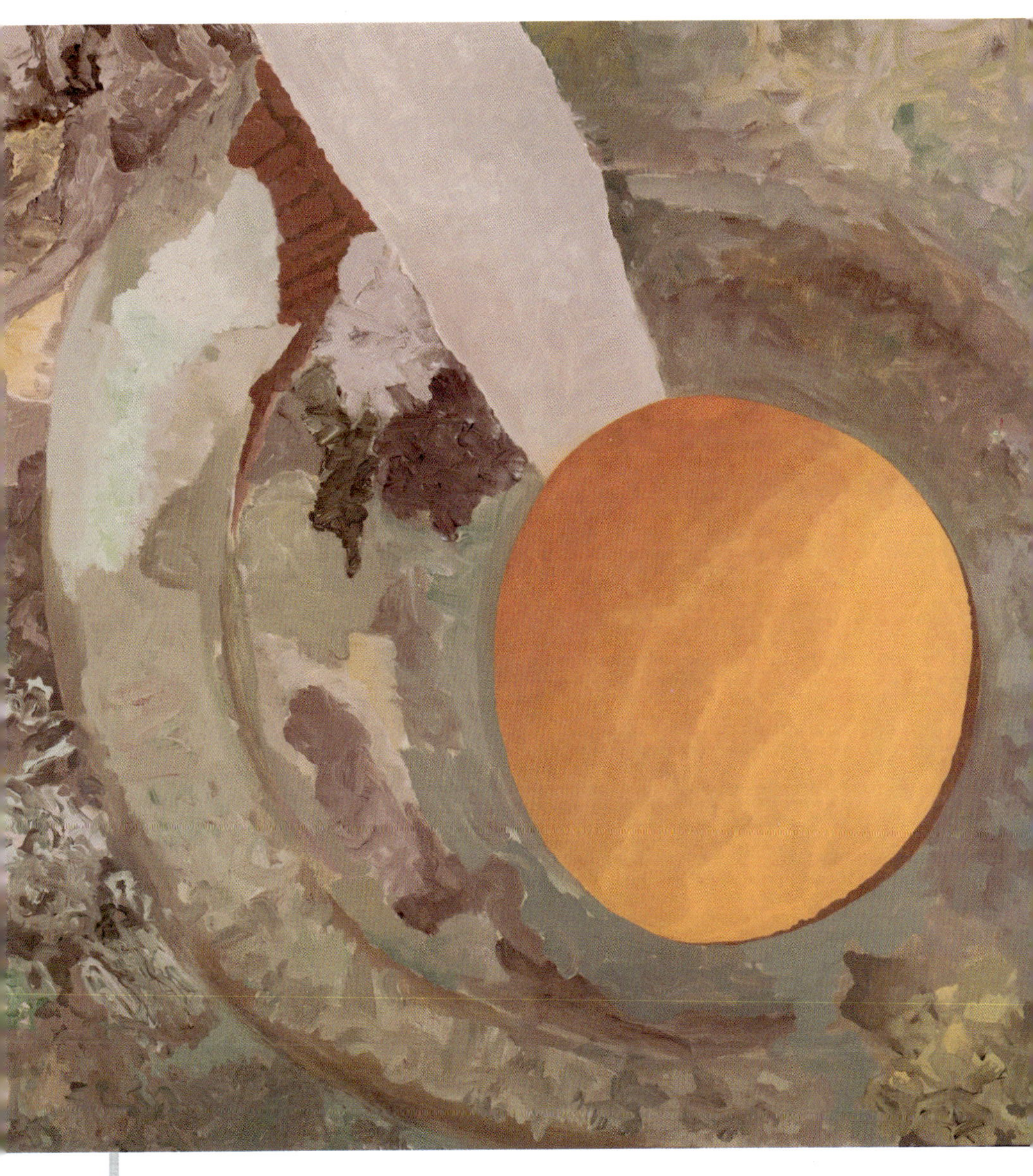

LOOKING INTO A WELL: EVENING DAZZLE (2014)

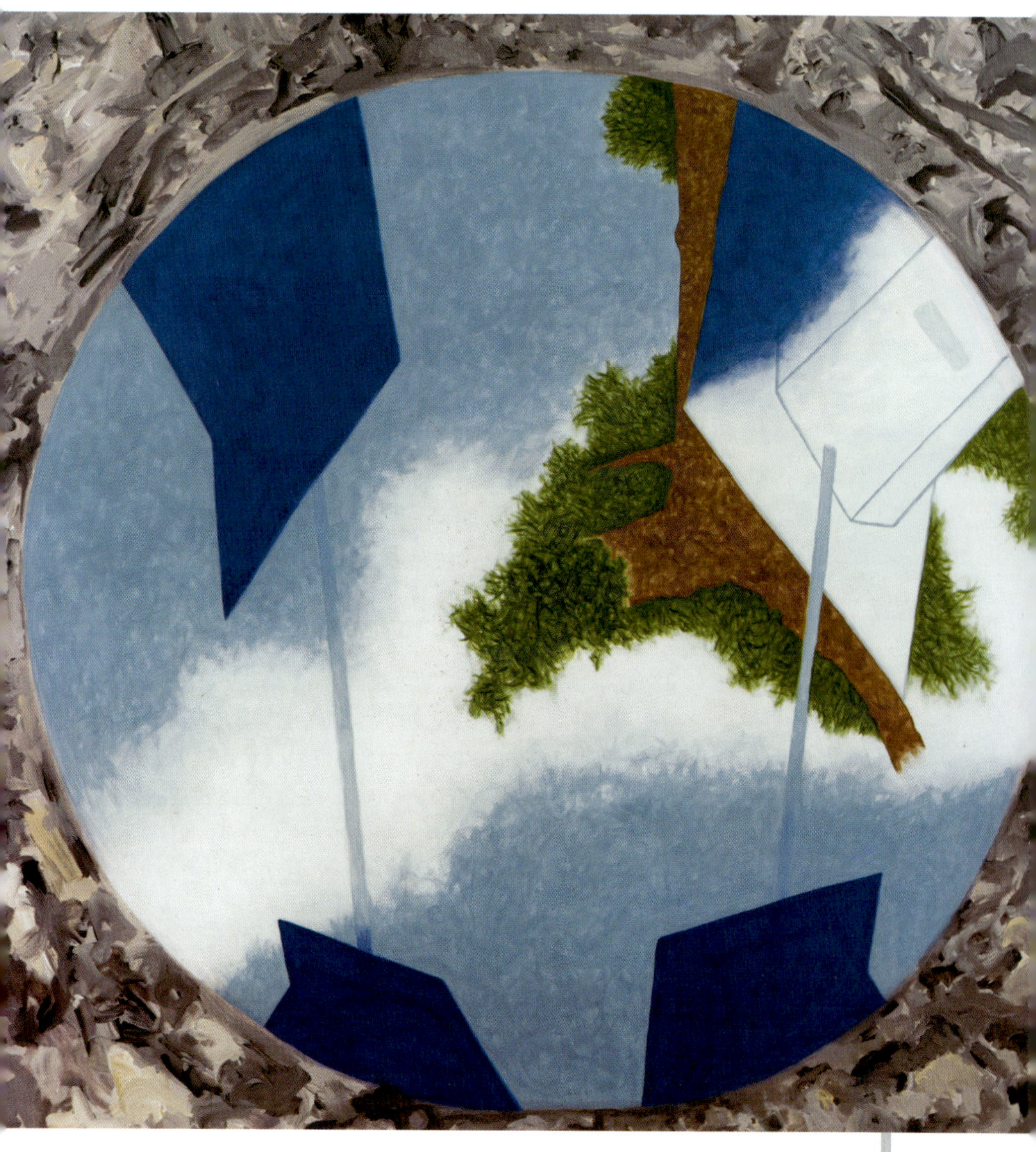

LOOKING INTO A WELL: FOUR PILLARS
(2015)

This gift for straddling apparent paradoxes, indeed for treating paradox as a bridge to be crossed, sustains his art, imparts to it a distinctive and memorable richness.

Bombay / Goa

February 2017–August 2018

Notes

Written in 1959, 'Urban' appeared in Nissim Ezekiel's fourth collection of poems, *The Unfinished Man* (1960). See Nissim Ezekiel, *Collected Poems 1952–1988* (New Delhi: Oxford University Press, 1989), p. 117. Ezekiel was a mentor, in different generations, to Gieve Patel and to the present author.

1   Ranjit Hoskote, 'The Startling View from the Studio: Recent Paintings by Gieve Patel and Sudhir Patwardhan' in *Gieve Patel | Sudhir Patwardhan* (New York: Bose Pacia/ BP Contemporary Art of India Series VOL. 28, 2006), p. 9.

2   See Ludwig Wittgenstein, *Philosophical Investigations* (Oxford: Blackwell, 1953).

3   Hoskote, 'The Startling View from the Studio', p. 9.

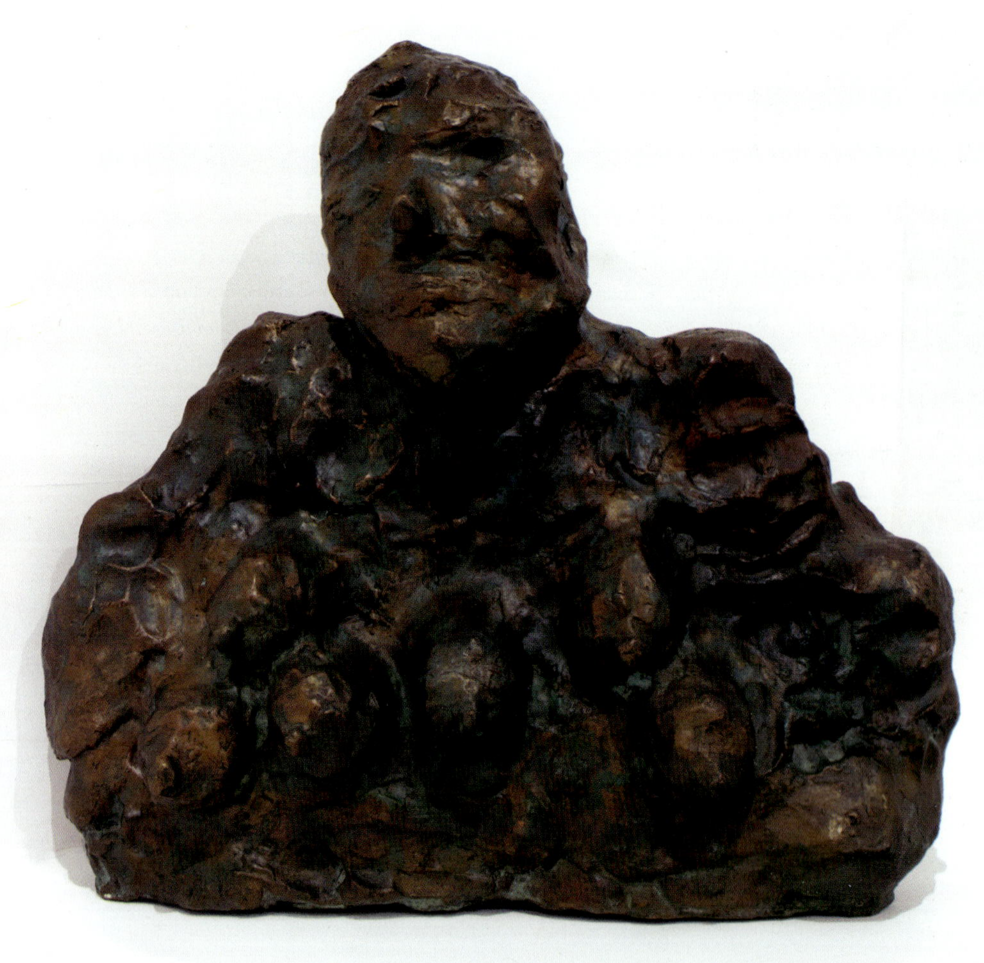

List of Illustrations

Acknowledgements

I would like to thank Arani and Shumita Bose of Bose Pacia, New York; Shireen Gandhy of Chemould Prescott Road (formerly Gallery Chemould), Bombay; Shalini H. Sawhney of the Guild Art Gallery, Alibaug & Bombay; Usha Mirchandani and Ranjana Steinruecke of Galerie Mirchandani + Steinruecke, Bombay; and Roshini Vadehra of the Vadehra Art Gallery, New Delhi.

The essays reproduced in this book originally appeared in exhibition catalogues published by these galleries:

–*An Economy of Violence* (Bombay: Gallery Chemould, 2000)

–*The Incarnate Particularity of Forms* (Bombay: Gallery Chemould & New Delhi: Vadehra Art Gallery, 2003)

–*The Startling View from the Studio* (Bose Pacia, 2006)

–*To Break and To Branch* (The Guild Art Gallery, 2007)

–*Sight as Covenant* (Bose Pacia, 2011)

–*Crossing the Bridge of Paradox* (Galerie Mirchandani + Steinruecke, 2018)

*

Special thanks are due to Ranjana Steinruecke and her team at Galerie Mirchandani + Steinruecke, Bombay, and to Shalini H. Sawhney and her team at the Guild Art Gallery, Alibaug and Bombay, for generously providing us with the images of the artist's work reproduced here; and Aparna Andhare for her untiring assistance with organizing the images.

*

To Nancy Adajania, my love and my eternal gratitude: this book emerges from the fabric of our life together, the friendship we shared with Gieve.

To Avaan Patel, my thanks for many years of friendship: this book is a tribute to her father, who touched many lives in poetry, the visual arts and theatre.

To Naveen Kishore, Sunandini Banerjee, Bishan Samaddar and Diven Nagpal at Seagull Books, dear sahridayas: thank you for so warmly embracing this book as a memorial tribute to Gieve, whose work was—and remains—significant to all of us.